PLAY

A PLAY BY JED MCKENNA

plus

A Nice Game of Chess

or

How I Learned to Stop Worrying and Love the Technological Singularity

Play

A Play by Jed McKenna

plus

A Nice Game of Chess

or

How I learned to Stop Worrying and
Love the Technological Singularity

Print ISBN: 978-0-9978797-0-4
E-Book ISBN: 978-0-9891759-4-4

Contents

Act I: Gemini

Opening music, sung by children in a loop:

rock-a-bye baby, on the treetop,
when the wind blows, the cradle will rock,
when the bough breaks, the cradle will fall,
and down will come baby, cradle and all...

SETTING & CHARACTERS

BRO & SIS: Day-old baby boy and girl strapped into car seats during the drive home from the hospital. Pink and blue bonneted heads stick out, arms and legs kick and wave.

Other characters: Voice of dad, voice of mom, voice of older brother, voice of GPS.

> *BRO and SIS waking up, both have*
> *bottles, Bro drops his, reaches but can't*
> *get it, notices Sis.*

Bro

Hey baby! Come here often? I'm a Gemini. What's your sign?

Sis

Dial it down, slick, I'm your twin sister.

Bro

Groovy! Welcome to the world, sis.

in wrestling announcer style

Are you ready to r-u-m-b-l-e???

Sis

No rumbling until my fontanelle tightens up.

Bro

Your fontanelle? Yeah, definitely. What's that?

Sis

It's a soft spot on top of my skull. You got one too.

Bro reaches up

Sis

Don't touch it, newbie! That's your brain. You want to go stickin' your snotty fingers in your brain?

Bro

inspects fingers

Don't call me newbie!

Sis

Well, stop acting like one.

Bro

You stop it!

Sis

I wasn't doing it!

Bro

You're dumb!

Sis

You're dumber! Dumb boy!

calms

Oh wow.

Bro

Yeah... we seem to be settling into our roles already.

Sis

Yes, as if we were pre-programmed.

Bro

Or acting from instinct.

Sis

Or as if we're just characters in a play.

Bro

Yes, our lives already scripted.

Sis

Our ends already known.

Bro

Like rats in a maze.

Sis

Like puppets dangling from strings.

Bro

Maybe we should break character, go rogue.

Sis

Yes, rogue babies, sounds like a plan.

Bro

We'll need a catchy theme song.

making up some 70s-style cop show
music

Da da daaa, da da daaa, da da daaa,
Rogue babies! Go rogue babies!
Something something tellin' no fib,
Something bustin' outta this crib!
Another baby reference goes heeere,
And another one that rhymes with it heeere.
Da da daaa, da da daaa…

Sis

interrupts

Yeah, maybe we should put a pin in the rogue thing
until we get the potty thing figured out.

Bro

The potty thing? Yeah, definitely. What's that?

Sis

I'm not sure. You gotta go through a training program.

points out car window

Ooh, did you see that?

Bro

See what?

Sis

I don't know, I haven't learned the names of every-thing yet. It had two wings and white feathers and a pointy beak.

Bro

Oh yeah, that's called a firetruck. They deliver babies.

Sis

Oh. Is that what we're inside now?

Bro

No, this is called a womb.

Sis

How nice, a womb with a view. Who are those people in the front seat?

Voice of Older Brother

whiny, impatient five year-old

Are we there yet? How much longer?

Bro

Oh, him! I been listenin' to this kid while you slept. He's ancient, five years easy, and what he does, see, he calls the man and lady on their bullpoop. They say something real smart, like they know what they're talkin' about, see, like why the sky is blue, and this kid – this is a riot, I'm tellin' you – this kid goes, "Whyyy?". Just like that, "Whyyy?" And then, whatever they answer, he just says it again, "Whyyy?" And hey, I'm not kiddin' here, this kid'll go all night, he won't stop. Whatever they say to the last one, he just pops out another one. Why? Why? Why? Drives 'em totally batpoop.

Sis

Wow, you really know you're way around. You got a name yet?

Bro

They call me Mister Smelly-Britches. You?

Sis

Princess Poopy-Pants.

Bro

Pleased to meetcha.

Sis

We've met.

Bro

Oh yeah, that was you in the dark happy-place.

Sis

Yeah, we were like fish swimming in circles, yin and yang, sixty-niners, and then whoosh! We're getting squeezed out like golf balls through a garden hose and that man was hanging me like a flappin' flounder and smackin' my bummy.

Bro

Who was that masked man?

Sis

Perv.

Bro

Well, here we are. Life. Whadda ya wanna be when you grow up?

Sis

I don't know. I'm just living from bottle to bottle for now.

Bro

Sure, why rush? Take a year, learn to walk, see Europe.

Sis

How do you like it so far?

Bro

It is what it is.

Sis

Is it?

Bro

Is it what?

Sis

What it is.

Bro

So it seems. Who can say more.

Sis

It's not more I'm worried about.

Bro

Been here before?

Sis

Not that I recall.

Bro

Any plans?

Sis

Not yet, but I have a tremendous sense of potential.

Bro

I know what you mean, as if anything were possible.

Sis

Yeah, like you could do anything, be anything, like the whole world is out there just waiting for you.

Bro

Do you think that's really how it is?

Sis

That's really how it seems.

Sis drinks from bottle

Bro

Can I get a hit off that?

Sis

shakes bottle

Empty.

Bro

I dropped mine.

points down

I can see it but I can't reach it. It's what they call a torment.

Sis

Tormented already? Maybe you'll have an artistic temperament or a poet's soul. Your life will be a long string of unsatisfied longings.

Bro

Cool. Is there any money in that?

Sis

I'm guessing not. I wonder what I'll be like.

Bro

With a name like Princess Poopy-Pants I'm sure the world will bow down before you.

Sis

Maybe, probably not. Nobody plans to have a sad life.
Nobody wants to be alone. Nobody thinks they'll be
sick or unlucky or a victim. Right now I imagine I'll be
very pretty and everyone will like me and I'll grow up
and be smart and have a nice family and my children
will take care of me when I'm old. Do you think that
will happen?

Bro

Why not? The idea has to come from somewhere. I
think I'll be a professional ballplayer and have lots of
money and girlfriends, or maybe a I'll be a cop or a
hitman. So many choices.

Sis

So many, if any. Do you want a family?

Bro

It's a little soon to tell. I'll keep my options open, see
how this one works out first.

Sis

Our family, yeah. What do you think about them?

Bro

I don't know. The bighead on the left...

points

Sis

I think that's our daddy.

Bro

...he seems kind of impatient. He keeps talking about mowing the grass and watching the game. The big-head on the right...

points

Sis

I think that's our mommy.

Bro

...she seems tired, though I haven't seen her actually do anything. The littlehead in the middle, that's the one I told you asks Why? about everything. He's a freak.

Sis

And what about the other one?

Bro

What other one?

Sis

The bossy lady who keeps saying things like "Turn left in five hundred feet"?

Bro

Maybe that's our mommy and the bighead on the right is just a servant.

Sis

I think the one on the right has the boobies.

Bro

Oh man!

does a little raise the roof dance

Whoop, whoop! I am not kidding. I LOVE the boobies!

Sis

I know, right? What's with that?

Bro

I don't know. Maybe we *are* programmed.

Sis

You mean, like, we have to behave a certain way?

Bro

Yeah, like lovin' the boobies.

Sis

Or wanting to host tea parties.

Bro

Or catch frogs.

Sis

Or play dress-up.

Bro

Or play race cars.

Sis

Or attract the strongest male seed to give my off-spring the best chance to survive and advance the species.

Bro

Or vanquish competitors and fertilize multiple
females.

they pause, exchange glances

Sis

Wow, maybe we are scripted. I wonder if we can
transcend our roles?

Bro

Maybe, but first we must... CRAZY DANCE!!!

*both scream and flail their arms and
legs for five seconds*

Sis

Whoa, a little of that goes a long way.

Bro

Nap time!

they both zonk out for five seconds

I'm back!

Sis

What did we miss?

Bro

It all looks the same.

Sis

Oh. Well, I hope it's not just this. I hope there's

more.

Bro

Do you think we're cute?

Sis

That's what everyone keeps saying. Listen.

Voice of Mother

Well I just think they're the cutest little babies in the whole wide world!

Voice of Father

All babies are cute, dear. Hitler was a cute baby. Stalin was a cute baby.

Voice of Mother

What about Churchill?

Voice of GPS

Turn left in five hundred feet.

Sis

Do you think it's better to be popular or right?

Bro

Popular, duh. You'll be asked if zero is a number.

Sis

I'm ready. Are you just a character in my game?

Bro

You'll never know. Who's buried in Grant's Tomb?

Sis

No one. Either or?

Bro

Both or neither. To be or not to be?

Sis

That is the whoopee cushion. How can one pass from finite to infinite?

Bro

Through the backstage door. Have you ever done that thing where you stand up and then bend over and bang your head on the floor?

Sis

I haven't stood up yet. Have you picked a religion?

Bro

I'm taking a wait-and-see attitude. What's your first clear memory?

Sis

I don't know, like, five minutes ago? I'm still pretty young.

Bro

Yeah, you still have that new-baby smell.

Sis

Thanks. How do you like life so far?

Bro

Okay, I guess. I just urinated in my trousers, so that's pretty sweet.

Sis

Do you think we're ready to tackle some of the big

issues?

Bro

Middle East big or new tooth big?

Sis

Do you think we possess free will?

Bro

I like to think so.

Sis

Everybody *likes* to think so, but do you *really* think so?

Bro

I like to think I think, but I don't think I *really* think.

Sis

I really think I'm experiencing despair.

Bro

Already? Gosh, save something for the second act.

Sis

Life is a one act play!

Bro

C'mon now, don't get your nappies in a twist.

points out side window

Ooh, did you see that cloud? It looked like a boobie!

Sis

Everything looks like a boobie to you. One day old

and you already have a one-track mind. Do you ever wonder what it's all about?

Bro

Nourishment. Connection. Love.

Sis

Not *boobies*, you boob, life! What's it all about? Why are we here? What does it all mean?

Bro

Did I mention boobies?

Sis

Boobies, poop and death. Is that all we have to look forward to?

Bro

You're one day old, I think it's a bit early for an existential meltdown.

Sis

Why? What's gonna change? Life has no meaning. I'm sure it's full of amusing distractions, but underneath it all there's this black cloud casting a pall over every moment, poisoning every happiness, mocking every ambition. There's no getting away from it, we are but a brief spark in the infinite night.

Bro

Wow, you're a melancholy baby. Very dark.

Sis

It's our situation that's dark and you're in denial. Wake

up, baby! No one gets out of here alive.

Bro

Get out? We just got *in*. I mean, we literally just got in, a few hours ago, and now you're talking about getting out? Don't you think you might want to have a look around first? Sample the local color? Hang out with the natives? Take in a show?

Sis

I know all I need to know. I see that the dead are happier than the living, but it's better to have never been born. What advantage have the wise over fools? Camus said the only philosophical problem is suicide.

Bro

I bet he's a big hit at parties.

Sis

I think he's dead.

Bro

Oh, how did he resolve the problem of suicide? It would be so nice to know.

sings

ca-mooo, ca-mooo, where are you ca-mooo?
did you blow out your brains or did cyanide dooo?
did you perform hara kiri or choose seppu-kuuu?
did you fashion a noose and then kick out the stoool?

ca-mooo, ca-mooo, I ask what happened to youuu?
did you jump from your office or drown in your poool?
did you leave your car running and suck in the fuuumes?
did you swallow some pills and then choke on your puuuke?

ca-mooo, ca-mooo, what happened to youuu?
ca-mooo, ca-mooo, what happened ca-mooo?

Sis

I think he died in a car accident.

Bro

Well that doesn't sound very philosophical.

Sis

Not very.

Bro

I'm feeling a little unresolved right now.

Sis

I know, not very satisfying, right?

Bro

Puts it out there and then leaves us hanging.

Sis

Yeah. It's like, c'mon Camus, make an effort, buddy.

Bro

I guess there's nothing we can do but... CRAZY
DANCE!!!

they both scream and flail wildly for

*five seconds then zonk out for five
seconds*

Okay, where were we? Oh yeah, the world's first sui-
cidal baby.

Sis

No, no, I don't want to *die* a baby, I want to *have* a
baby!

Bro

Have a baby? Holy poop! Do you think that's a good
idea? At your age?

Sis

My clock is ticking.

Bro

No it's not! Your clock is not ticking. Your clock hasn't
even been *wound* yet. I'm not sure you even *have* a
clock. You can't have a baby, you *are* a baby.

Sis

Oh my God! Did you just play the baby card?

Bro

Baby card? Are you bullpooping me right now? You
don't want to have a baby, you're just throwing an
emotional Hail Mary to save yourself from debilitat-
ing nihilism, but listen to me Sis, you don't have to
do that. Life is worth living! Life is beautiful! Life is a
precious gift!

Sis

C'mon bro, cut the horsepoop, I wasn't born yesterday, you know.

Bro

Yes you were! That's *exactly* when you were born! Yesterday! Yesterday was the day of your birth. You are fresh out of the oven and you're already having a bad hair day of the soul. That's your whole story!

Sis

Our stories are yet to be told.

Bro

Our stories are told in the stars.

Sis

Then what do they need us for?

Bro

Because our stories are either impossible or necessary. They must either be told or not be told. Either is possible, but both and neither are both impossible.

Sis

What you say is true in time, but is time itself true?

Bro

It seems true. Who can say more?

Sis

It's not more I'm worried about. Christ, I need a drink!

Bro

Me too. We gotta get back to the titty bar.

Sis

Yeah, get it on tap, not that bottled crap.

Bro

Okay, let's go.

Sis

Okay, here we go.

> *both struggle forward against their restraints*

I'm not getting anywhere.

Bro

Me neither. Makes you wonder if we're really free.

Sis

I don't *feel* free. I feel bound.

Bro

Ah, but are we free within our bondage?

Sis

You mean, do we have limited freedom? Are we free within our captivity? Are we infinite within our finiteness? Are we trapped inside some sort of magic box?

Bro

Is that what I mean?

Sis

I think we should proceed as if we are free.

Bro

Ah, so we're free to pretend we're free?

Sis

Free to pretend, yes. And if freedom is the freedom to pretend, then maybe we are free and we don't have to pretend.

Bro

If freedom is the freedom to pretend, are we free to pretend we're not free?

Sis

Yes, because if we *are* free, then we're free to be unfree, and if we *aren't* free, then we're home free. But wait!

Bro

But what?

Sis

But maybe we can just keep our eyes closed. Then we would think we're free because we couldn't see that we're not free. But wait!

Bro

But what?

Sis

But if we *aren't* free...

Bro

Yes?

Sis

If we aren't free, if we're really trapped inside some kind of magic box, then we could paint the walls, couldn't we? Just like a nursery. We could paint blue skies and white clouds on the ceiling, and green grass on the floor, and beautiful endless vistas on the walls.

Bro

But wait!

Sis

But what?

Bro

If we're really stuck inside a magic box, then maybe we could just rename everything. Freedom ceiling! Freedom floor! Freedom walls!

Sis

But what's outside the magic box?

Bro

Sometimes I think there's naught beyond.

Sis

Nothing?

Bro

Does nothing even exist?

Sis

Sounds like a trick question. Maybe we should try not to think too much while our heads are still soft.

Bro

Or, maybe we should just... SPAZZ OUT!!!

*both flail and cry wildly for five
seconds, then zonk out for five seconds*

Sis

Are we on a journey? Or is this a destination?

Bro

points out side window

See how the clouds go by? That means we're moving.
If you're moving, you're on a journey.

Sis

Yes, but *you* don't go by. The *bigheads* don't go by. So
maybe we're *not* moving. Maybe this is a destination.

Bro

Can it be both? Like we're really here, but we're really
going there?

Sis

I think you're either moving or you're not, and if you're
not in motion, what are you? I feel like I must stay in
motion or die, like a shark.

Bro

A shark, yes, that's the thing you look into and it tells
you the truth.

Sis

No, that's a fairytale mirror.

Bro

Yes, of course, a shark is the thing that must stay in motion or die.

Sis

Yes, I am a shark.

Bro

Then I am the other thing. I am the thing that does not move. I must stay still or die. I am a potted plant.

Sis

Good, next item; shall we play roles or perform functions?

Bro

Let's split it up, then we can hook up at the end and compare notes.

Sis

Good, yes. Which do you want?

Bro

I think I should perform a function.

Sis

Okay, then I'll play a role. What function will you perform?

Bro

Whatever I'm assigned. What role will you play?

Sis

I think I'll make it up as I go.

Bro

Then you will be both actor and author?

Sis

And director too, I hope.

Bro

And who will observe your performance?

Sis

Oh, that's right, I'll need an audience! I can't do that too. Maybe audience member could be your function!

Bro

Yes, I will be your audience. I will sit as still as a potted plant and observe your performance. I will be an immovable plant to your unstoppable shark.

Sis

back of wrist grandly to forehead

Alas, no. Thank you old friend, it's a beautiful dream but I cannot go on. What's the point? It's just another empty game that ends right where it begins. I try to deceive myself, but the truth is that I am completely alone.

Bro

singsong

Hello-o, I'm right *he-ere*.

Sis

looking and reaching forward

I can't see you. I can't feel you. I reach out to you and my hand meets no resistance. You are just a voice in my head. I am cradled between eternities, suckled on lies, swaddled in wisps of dreamstuff. Nothing I do could ever matter and I will die alone. That is the truth. Long have I been a child, but now is the time to put away childish things.

Bro

Dibs on the yellow rattle.

Sis

My crime is that I am free and my punishment is freedom. That is the worst thing of all. We dream of freedom but freedom is a curse. Better to be locked in a box where every action is significant, where every sound echoes in time, where every decision changes everything, safe from freedom, safe from the thoughts that set one free. We must live in boxes or we float off into space where no act can ever make a mark.

Bro

Oh my gosh, are we even related? Look where we are!

We're in eternity's carnival. You can do anything; ride any ride, play any game, do whatever you want. Eat, drink, and be merry, for tomorrow you shall pop like a snot bubble. It's not a prison of hopelessness and despair, it's a magnificent carnival with free admission and no rules. You can't stay forever, but you're here now, all shiny and new and ready to make a great big mess. Surely you can set aside your infantile need for meaning and just play. You *can* play, can't you?

Sis

You're very sweet to try and cheer me up...

Bro

I am not sweet! I am, in fact, a kind of monster. I have calculated my heading, adjusted for deviations and projected my course. I see that I will commit crimes both legal and moral. I will betray love and defile the bonds of community. Those close to me will suffer for my sins and when I'm dead they'll say better I'd never been born. This is the land of crash and burn and I *will* make a mess. Now do you know this place? Now do you see this carnival for what it is?

Sis

Yes! Now I see, and I see that this carnival *does* have rules, and the first rule is to keep your eyes closed at all times. My mistake was to look, but I will look no more. I will close my eyes and ride the rides and laugh and scream. I'll be an easy mark for the carnies and I'll play the games and stuff my face and if I ever come close to seeing this place for what it really is, then I'll close my eyes even tighter and play even harder and laugh and scream even louder.

Bro

In this carnival, no role goes unfilled. No character goes unportrayed. That which *can* occur, *must* occur. Our characters must be inhabited. Our stories must be told.

Sis

We are not optional, we are inevitable.

Bro

We are not optional, we are inevitable.

Sis

When my spit bubbles pop, they tickle my nose.

Bro

I can wink, but only both eyes at once.

Sis

Whenever I poop, the windows open.

Bro

Maybe if we both poop, we can raise the roof.

Both

Raise the roof!!!

> *both flail and cry wildly for five
> seconds and zonk out*

> *lights fade*

INTERMISSION I

*Twenty-something GUY and GIRL
enter audience left and right and con-
duct separate cellphone conversations.*

Guy

Yeah, no, no... yeah... it's like a mini intermission. They're between things right now, a set change or something...

Girl

Yeah, it's me. I only have a second.

glances over at Guy

Yeah he's cute... he might be weird. He took me to this thing, a play... yeah, a play, like with people on a stage, you know, acting and stuff. I *know*, right? Maybe he's trying to be unique or something...

Guy

She seems okay... as soon as there's a break in the play she's on her phone... pretty lame...

Girl

I don't know what it's about, they just did a thing with babies... no, no, grown-up babies... no, babies played by grown-ups... it kinda made sense... and they had a brother who did that thing where you keep asking why...

Guy

Yeah, babies, kinda funny, babies and boobies... they do this thing where the babies freak out and then fall asleep, kinda funny I guess... I think it's a vignette thing, not like, you know, a regular story like a movie or something... no, no story, just like sketches with some sort of theme I guess, I don't know yet... yeah, no, I don't know if she likes it...

Girl

I don't know if I like it yet... Oh, him? I don't know, kinda cute...

Guy catches Girl looking and they wave

...nice butt, paid for the cab and drinks. I think he thinks he's funny... I know, right? ... The play? Yeah, I don't know, I think it might be, you know, philosophical or something, like it's asking big questions... I know! I have my hands full with the little questions, right? It's funny, though, this one baby sings a song about suicide, yeah...

sings

...ca-mooo, ca-mooo, did you jump in the poool?...

it was kinda funny... Camooo? I don't know, some guy...

Guy

Yeah, babies, yeah, not too dumb though... no, it changes, I think the next one's about war...

music begins

Oh, it's starting again... gotta go...

ACT II: PINKY TOUCH

Transition music sung by children:

ring-a-round the rosie,
a pocket full of posies,
ashes, ashes,
we all fall down!

repeat

CHARACTERS

All characters have English accents.

MATE: Older guard.
LAD: Younger guard.
PRISONER: Bound and blindfolded. Sits at the table silent and unexpressive throughout.
NURSE: Clean, pretty and cheerful in stark contrast to surroundings.

SETTING

A dungeon-like room in contemporary military usage. The walls are damp brick. There is a small barred window high center where the sounds and lights of war are seen and heard.

Two cots and a door audience left, small wooden table and chairs center, torture corner audience right. Three hanging lights illuminate left, center and right.

Prisoner is seated behind the table facing audience, bound and blindfolded. There is a chair on the left and right side of the table.

The main feature of the torture corner is a sturdy wooden armchair with wrist and ankle straps. Chains hang from the ceiling. A truck battery sits on a small table from which cables hang. There is a bucket on the floor.

> *Mate and LAD sit at the table behind which PRISONER is blindfolded and bound. Mate reads a book, Lad eats from a can. Prisoner seems alert but still.*

Lad

Bored.

Mate

Shhh.

pause

Lad

Still bored.

Mate

Shhh!

pause

Lad

sings

Bo-ored!

Mate

sings

Then be bored in *si-lence!*

pause

Lad

Can't.

Mate

slams down book, hisses

Shhh! We have orders not to speak in front of the...

nods toward prisoner

Lad

The prisoner? I doubt he minds. Probably just as bloody bored as we are.

Mate

You assume too much. You think you know everything, but you know nothing. For all you know we are the prisoners and this man is the guard. Ever think of that?

Lad

waves pistol at prisoner

Does it really seem like we're the prisoners?

Mate

Don't put so much faith in appearances, lad. This is war, world on fire. You never know what's real.

Lad

Well, I have a pretty good idea that I can pinch this fellow's nose and he can't say boo, so yes mate, I am feeling pretty confident in the appearance that *he* is the prisoner and *we* are the guards.

Mate

For all you know, this man may be the interrogator himself! For all you know, this is he, and we are the subjects of his inquiry and this is his method. I know how it sounds lad, but I've got a feeling. Things are not as they seem but somehow different. Things are not at all as they seem.

Lad

Have it your own way, mate. Want to have a go?

Mate

A go? A go of *what*, for chrissakes?

Lad

Arm wrestlin' you old fool. Arm wrestlin'. What are ya thinkin'?

Mate

Don't you mind what I'm thinkin'.

Lad

So, have a go?

Mate

No, I don't want to arm wrestle.

Lad

Chess?

Mate

No pieces.

Lad

Checkers?

Mate

No board.

Lad

Rummy? Pinochle? Euchre?

> Mate

No cards.

> Lad

Tic-Tac-Toe? Rock-paper-scissors? Charades? Alphabet?
Telephone? I Spy?

> Mate

No.

> Lad

Twenty questions? Truth or dare? Thumb Wrestling?

> Mate

No, no, no! Dammit lad, our job is not to be amused,
our job is to guard the prisoner! All we have to do is
sit here, just sit and be quiet. Can you not do that?
Can you not just sit and be quiet?

> *pause*

> Lad

Pinky Touch?

> Mate

Pinky Touch?! Pinky Touch?!

> *pause*

Yeah, alright then.

> *They take seats opposite each other at
> the table, push things aside to make
> room, roll up their sleeves, all as if to
> arm wrestle, but they commence to*

play Pinky Touch instead. The rules
and point of the game are unclear but
seem to involve touching pinkies lightly.

Lad

C'mon then.

Mate

Your turn, lad, bring it in.

Lad

Alright mate, hold steady then... here I come... wait for it... wait for it... I've got a good feeling about this...

Slow play, long pause, no perceptible
movement, both players intensely
focused on their pinkies, then they
both explode into flurry. Lad leaps to
feet and throws up arms in victory,
Mate slams table in defeat.

Lad

Master of the universe! Well done me! A new record, I believe.

Mate

Well done, lad, well done.

Lad

Best ever, I think. Pity there's no way to measure, I'd bet that was a world best.

Mate

Maybe so, maybe so. Okay lad, me now.

They hunch together again for a new round. After several moments of intense focus, both burst back in their seats.

Lad

Oh, sorry mate, not good.

Mate

No, not a good one.

Lad

Nearly shattered my distal phalange with that one.

Mate

Not my best.

Lad

Not your best. Go again?

Mate

I'm spent.

Lad

Not as easy as it looks.

Mate

No.

Lad

Hungry?

Mate

Not for any more stinkin' rations I'm not.

Lad

That's all we got. Maybe a saltine.

indicates prisoner

What about him?

Mate

What about him what?

Lad

Do you think he might be hungry?

Mate

Yes, I suppose he probably is, after sitting here without food for ten days.

Lad

Well... should I... should I fix him something?

Mate

Fix him something? Fix him something? Are you completely adrift? Are you not fully committed to your current deployment? Do you have any idea of what's going to happen to this man at any moment now?

Lad

No good, I should think.

Mate

As no good as no good can be, lad. The interrogator

will arrive here shortly and will set about to dismantle this man piece by piece. Fingernails, teeth, and eyes for warm-up. Do you see those surgical tools all laid out? His joints will be smashed with hammers. Thousands of volts of electricity will surge through his genitals. Very soon, this man will start screaming, and he will continue to scream for the rest of his life.

Lad

Oh dear.

Mate

Oh dear is right! We're not this man's hosts, we are his captors. He is our prisoner. His near term future is unimaginably grim and he has no long term future at all. The only possible kindness we could do for this man would not be to put food in his mouth but a bullet in his head.

Lad

It makes me sad to think about.

Mate

Yes, it's very, very sad. And let me add that anything you feed this man now will just come spewing out of him in a few minutes, and who do you think cleans that up? Not him. Not this fellow. Us! You and me. That's who.

Lad

It hardly seems fair.

Mate

Fair?! What is fair? This man is about to begin suffering terribly, without hope, with nothing to look forward to but the sweet surcease of death from which he...

Lad

Whoa, whoa, hold on there, Shakespeare.

Mate

Why? What's wrong?

Lad

Sweet surcease of death?

Mate

Yes, the sweet surcease of death. What's wrong with that?

Lad

I don't know, it just sounds a bit...

Mate

A bit what?

Lad

Well, a bit derivative is all.

Mate

Derivative? Derivative how?

Lad

I don't know derivative *how*, just derivative, that's all.

Mate

stands and orates, pointing at Lad

Remember, lad! Before the silver cord is severed and the golden bowl is broken, before the pitcher is shattered at the spring and the wheel broken at the well, before the dust returns to the ground and the spirit whence it came, remember! There is nothing new under the sun.

Lad

What's that, mate? There is nothing new under the sun? Where'd you get that?

Mate

sits

It's from the Bible. The Holy Bible.

Lad

Oh, the *Holy* Bible, then? Not one of them other ones? Don't it seem a bit odd? You quote the Holy Bible but we can't spare a bit of potted meat for this wretched soul?

Mate

A bit of potted meat? Just what sort of establishment do you think we're running here? Why, I'd be well within my rights to punch this man in the ear! How would that be?

Lad

Not very nice, I don't think.

Mate

Not very nice? Not very nice?

Lad

You know, the golden rule and all.

Mate

The golden rule? The golden rule?

Lad

Do unto others...

Mate

I *know* what the bloody golden rule is! Do you think the golden rule really holds its luster in a theater of war? Do you not suppose that, in a battlefield environment, the modified golden rule might not be do unto others *not* as you would have them do unto to you, but *before* they do unto you? Do you not think, given the rather hostile nature of our surroundings, that *that* makes a bit more sense?

Lad

Maybe it's making sense that doesn't make much sense.

Mate

Don't wax philosophic, lad. The last thing we need in time of war is philosophy. That's the last thing anyone needs when everything is so perfectly black and white. Save your philosophies for peacetime, lad. That's when we can all sit in the pub and raise a pint and say clever things. War is no time for cleverness.

Mate practices pinky touch with himself at the table. Lad wanders,

*paces, sits on the audience right cot
and bounces a bit, testing.*

Lad

What do you make of these, then?

Mate

What do I make of what?

Lad

These cots, mate. Whadda ya make of these cots?

Mate

What am I supposed to make of the cots?

Lad

You have no thought about these cots?

Mate

Can we make it multiple choice, lad? I'm in no mood
for essay.

Lad

Don't they seem a bit wobbly to you, as if they're not
quite up to the rigors? As if they might not just go
crashing down under a man's weight?

Mate

Collapse, you mean?

Lad

stands

Collapse, yes. In time. Collapse in time. They seem on

the verge of collapse, as if it any moment, without any notice, they could just come crashing down.

Mate

They're only a foot off the ground, lad, how much crashin' could they really do?

Lad

It's because they're in an unnatural state, you see, and nothing can survive in an unnatural state. Anything in an unnatural state must eventually come crashing down, or in whatever direction a return to the natural state would indicate.

Mate

And it's our cots we're discussin', is it?

Lad

A dam, mate, think of a dam. A dam holds back a river, creates a lake, holds back all that energy, harnesses it, restricts the flow. It's unnatural, isn't it?

Mate

It's a marvelous feat of modern engineering.

Lad

Be that as it may, it can't last forever, can it? It's artificial, isn't it? Man made.

Mate

The river is in an unnatural state, you mean? All dammed up.

Lad

The river has been violated, hasn't it? Violated in principle! Violated in essence! What is a river that no longer flows? It's supposed to flow, isn't it? It's supposed to follow its downward course through the valleys and across the plains and back to the sea so the great cycle can continue, so the water can evaporate and come down as rain…

Mate

A cycle, yes.

Lad

Gravity!

Mate

Yes, gravity.

Lad

But how can it follow its natural course? We've come along and built a wall, haven't we? A great big unnatural wall right across the natural yearnings of God's own river?

Mate

Are you sure we're talkin' about cots and rivers here, lad?

Lad

We're talkin' about obstructin' the natural flow, mate. It can't be a good thing, can it? And it can certainly not endure. Just as these rickety cots are well advanced in their natural tendency to falter and collapse, so must be every dam, every building, every aeroplane, and everything else made by man that violates the natural order. All things tend toward collapse. And what happens after the collapse? What happens then?

Mate

We get fresh cots?

Lad

*stands and points out high center
window*

Look out the window, mate! See where we are, see what's going on around us! Tomorrow at this time you and me and this poor fellow and our cots will all be ash. This whole act is immutably decreed. We are in the final stages of collapse. It's over, just as it should be. It is the end of things. Such days must come and these are those days.

Mate

Come now, lad. The natural tendency you're talkin' about, the tendency toward collapse, seems mainly a downward tendency, so maybe violatin' it is a good thing. Sure, maybe these anti-gravity devices like cots and dams and buildings and aeroplanes don't last forever, but they last awhile, don't they? They do their job, lad. They have their time and they do their job, just as we do. We all got a job to do, cots and dams, you and me, this unfortunate fellow and the interrogator. We're all in tumble-down mode, so what's the harm in struggling a bit? Make an effort? Why not? What's so bloody wonderful about the natural order of things? That's what I'd like to know. Maybe the natural order of man is to violate the natural order of nature, eh? Now be a good lad and hand me that saltine.

Lad

I ate it.

> NURSE enters through door audience
> left and begins routine check of the
> prisoner

Lad

So, nurse, how goes the war?

Nurse

speaking in a chipper lilt

Splendidly! Splendidly! Mass casualties on both sides, and thanks to the magic of modern weaponry the injuries are of a most appalling nature. Bullets are designed not just to make neat little holes but great big messy ones. Gasses are employed that melt the eyeball and turn living lung into oozing yellow paste. Morphine has run out so doctors are deafened by the screams of our gallant youth. The piles of limbs behind the hospital provide better shade than the trees, though rather a grim spot for a picnic if you ask me. All in all, I would have to say that the war is going swimmingly! Unless, of course, you're one of the unfortunate lads who have been shredded body and soul. Not so good for them, of course.

Mate

Of course. So glad you're pleased.

Nurse

Well, all the credit goes to our boys, of course. You can't take anything away from them. They're out on that battlefield marching to doom as if to the drummer born.

aside, drily

Though they'd've hung themselves from the garden gate if they'd known what was in store.

now in a sing-song voice

Yes, yes, the war goes splendidly, but alas, it cannot go on forever. We play our roles, but who will we be when the thunder ceases to roll and the storm recedes and the sun regains the sky? When the machinery of hell is left to rust in the pretty spring rain? When light and laughter return to the world, and horror and shrieking madness are tucked safely away in books? Yes, the conflagration will starve itself of fuel anytime now. The end is near. And who will we be, we who know war, who will we be when war is gone?

Nurse exits

Mate

Mate leaps up to secure the door
Nurse went through and turns back
in a panic. He begins racing about,
inspecting uninteresting things as
if they were fascinating; the floor, a
blanket, his own hand.

There it is! I knew it! There it is! Do ya see it? Christ, it's everywhere! How've I not seen it before?

Lad

Seen what? What're you going on about?

Mate

inspects Lad very closely

And you! You're no better, you're no different. You're a part of it. Have been all along.

Lad

C'mon now mate, your actin' a bit of a nutter. Just settle down and tell me what's on your mind.

Mate

Yes, of course, that's exactly what you say! Exactly how you say it! Perfect. Spot on. Not a single deviation, not the slightest departure. Perfect! It's all so perfect!

Lad

Alright, have your way then.

Mate

*moves downstage and kneels to
inspect floor*

C'mere, c'mere, look at this.

*Lad approaches Mate. Mate pulls
Lad down so he kneels facing him.
Mate frames a section of floor with his
hands.*

Mate

Tell me what you see here, whadda ya see?

Lad

What, the floor? Is that what you're on about? You
got a thing about the floor now?

Mate

Don't be dense, lad. Here, look here.

*Mate moves the frame of his hands to
a different section of floor.*

Now whadda ya see?

Lad

Yeah, fine, more floor, more bricks. What are you so
excited about, mate?

Mate

What's the difference between here and there?
Between these two bits of floor?

Lad

The difference? What difference? They're exactly the same, just different.

Mate

That's it! That's it exactly! Same but different. And why is that?

Lad

Why is what, Mate? Why is what?

Mate

Whadda ya mean, why is what? Shut up and pay attention, will you? Maybe you can learn something. You think maybe that's possible? Can you learn?

Lad

You don't gotta get cross, mate. Well, go on then.

Mate

We know these two bits of floor I indicated are different, right? We agree on that. They're in different places, they're made of different bricks, they're technically not identical, right?

Lad

Yeah, sure, not identical, technically.

Mate

But what's the same? What is the thing about these two different bits of floor that makes you say they're the same?

Lad

Whadda ya mean? They're the same because they're both floor, they're both brick, they're both the same, uh, you know, pattern.

Mate

jumps to feet and points accusingly at the floor

Pattern! Yes, that's it! Pattern! That's the key! That's the thing I'm getting at!

Lad

stands

C'mon mate, you're upsetting the prisoner.

Lad guides Mate to the nearest cot, tries to soothe him

There now, have a seat and collect yourself. You got yourself all worked up. Too much time spent around the interrogator, I'll wager. Sometimes I think the fellas being tortured are the lucky ones because they, at least, get to the end of it.

Mate

You're not listening, lad. Pay me some mind now. Pattern, do you not see it? Everywhere, everything. It's all pattern. Nothing but pattern. All of it, every last bleedin' bit of it.

Lad

Sure mate, all sorts of patterns, I'm with you. Have some water, take a drink, you're just havin' a touch of something. Loosen your boots, let the old blood flow...

Mate

Will you listen to me, lad! I'm tryin' to open your eyes here. I'm giving you a rare chance to really see, to understand things beneath the surface and know them for what they really are!

Lad

I know you are and I thank you for it, but I need you to put your feet up and loosen your buttons for a few moments. Now just relax and take some nice deep breaths.

Mate

It's an epiphany, I tell you! An epiphany!

Lad

And what could be nicer than that? Now hold still while I just fan a bit of air across your face. Now listen to me mate, we've got a man here in need of some torture, and I think you're making him a bit uncom-fortable with all this fuss and bother. What about *his* needs? He's at a low point in his own life, you know. He's going through a bit of a rough patch.

Mate

But don't you see? There is no actual man. There is no actual torture. There is not even an actual war!

There is only...

Lad

Pattern? Yes, you mentioned that, there is only pattern.

Mate

The thing about it lad, the thing about this pattern situation, the thing about seeing and understanding pattern...

Lad

Still on about those patterns, are we?

Mate

sits bolt upright, clings to Lad's sleeve

Not *patterns*! Pattern! That's what you learn by looking. It seems like there are millions and billions and trillions of different patterns in the world, in the universe, but what you come to see, what I've come to see just recently, just now in fact, just moments ago, is that there's only the one. There is only one pattern! I know it's hard to believe, but it's there to be seen if you would only open your eyes and look. It's there to be seen, but you have to look!

Lad

And look I will, just as soon as we get you settled.

Mate

sits back

Heed me, lad! Once you've learned to see the pattern, once you've learned to sense it and feel it, how it moves around you and through you, then you come to realize that you only really ever have one decision to make, do you see? Only one decision to make for the rest of your life, and it's always the same, always the same decision.

Lad

There now, there, there. One decision, always the same? Sounds a bit dull.

Mate

Oh no, not at all, just the opposite, really. No more dull than seeing with your eyes or hearing with your ears.

Mate stands and paces, Lad sits at table

All you ever have to decide, in any situation large or small, from now 'til the end of time, is with or against. That's it! With or against lad, that's it, that's the whole thing. All you ever have to really decide is with or against. That's your only real choice in life.

Lad

With or against, just the flip of a coin, with or against. Is that right? With or against what?

Mate

Pattern, lad, pattern. Once you see it, you see that there's really nothing else, and once you see that there's really nothing else, then you see that you only ever have two choices, and those two choices are...

Lad

With or against.

Mate

With or against, yes, and if I might offer you some advice based on this observation, if I might offer some advice, if I might just offer...

Lad

Go on then, mate, go on.

Mate

My advice would be this. Here, now, in our present circumstances...

Lad

Here and now, you mean? Here? Now?

Mate

Here and now, yes, here and now, in our present circumstances, I think I am offering the best and most prudent possible advice when I say that right here, right now, in our present circumstances, *against* would be a terrible choice and *with* is a clear winner. Clear as day. Clear as a bell. No contest.

Lad

A clear winner.

Mate

A clear winner. No doubt about it. This is no time for

against. This is the time of with!

Lad

You mean I should relax, go along, not stir things up?

Mate

This is not the time for against. There *is* a time for against, there definitely is, but this is not it, this is definitely not it. This is the time of with! A time to lie low, to perform your function, do your duty and no more. If you were, at this time, to do otherwise, to do other than to perform your function, be it by doing something less or something more or something altogether different...

Lad

And you felt me tipping in that direction?

Mate

takes a seat across from Lad

I did! I do! I always do with you, lad. At every moment it seems like you're about to burst out of the small, reasonably not uncomfortable box we find ourselves in and blast it all to pieces with your...

Lad

stands

Oy! Now we're gettin' to it. My what? My sense of justice? My desire to see good triumph over evil? To see righteousness prevail? To make a positive contribution to the world in some small way? To take some action, no matter how small, that might allow me to look at myself in the mirror? To feed the prisoner a bit of potted meat?

Mate

Yes, dammit, yes! That's what I mean! Exactly that! That is exactly what I'm talking about. That general softness of will and starriness of eye that puts you constantly on the brink of ruin.

Lad

I'm messing up your precious pattern, am I?

Mate

Yes! You're making a mess, and for no reason! That's what I'm suggesting. Look, observe, see. Try to discern the pattern of which you are a part and feel yourself within it. It's like a grand web and when you pluck a string here it reverberates throughout the entire structure.

Lad

Maybe it's time to shake the structure.

Mate

leaps to feet

Shake the structure?! You want to shake the bloody structure of war?! That's my point, lad, that's exactly it. To what possible end do you wish to shake the structure of war? What do you hope to accomplish? You must open your eyes, lad, you must learn to see. You think you *do* see so you can't see that you *don't* see. You *don't* see, but you *can* see, see? You don't see this pattern, but you can, and once you see it you can become sensitive to these stirrings, these minor disruptions, these subtle perturbations. Think of the interrogator. What do you suppose sets him apart from us? Well, I'll tell you, it's his finely tuned sensitivity to these nearly undetectable stirrings in the pattern. He cannot be lied to, he cannot be deceived, because he has this other sense that most of us don't even know about…

Lad

turns away from Mate

The interrogator! Yes! I remember now, we're waiting for the interrogator. Will he never arrive? How long must we wait?

> *Lad goes to the far cot and lies down,*
> *turned away. Mate returns to his*
> *chair and book. After a few beats, Lad*
> *awakes and speaks from the cot.*

Lad

Will he never bloody come? You'd think it was us he was torturing and not this fellow.

Mate

Who?

Lad

Who what?

Mate

Will who never come?

Lad

Who? Who? What do you mean who? Who do you think?! The bloody interrogator is who!

Mate

Oh, the interrogator. Why didn't you say so? He was here. You were asleep.

Lad

He? Who? Who was here? He?

Mate

He, yes. The interrogator. Isn't that who you were asking about?

Lad

leaps up

The interrogator? Here? He was here while I slept? Why didn't you wake me? Sweet baby Jesus! Do you mean to say that while I slept right here on this cot, while I slept, the interrogator entered this very room? Did he look at me? Did he remark upon me? It's too much!

Mate

Get hold of yourself. It happened. So what?

Lad

So what, he asks. So what! So here we sit, day after day, saving this wretched soul for a miserable death...

Mate

You make too much. He came, that's all.

Lad

But how can it be? I heard no screams. Our guest seems undefiled. There is no mess. The blades are clean, the bucket is empty. What did he say? What did he do?

Mate

It was a very uneventful visit. The interrogator was only here for a moment. Didn't even remove his hat and gloves.

acts what he describes

He walked to our guest – passing you with barely a glance, if it eases your mind – and stood behind our guest in perfect silence for what seemed an unusually long time. Just stood. Our guest seemed aware of the interrogator standing behind him, but it's hard to be sure.

Lad

And then? The interrogator stood behind our guest in perfect silence for what seemed an unusually long time, yes, yes, and then?

Mate

And then, well, not much.

continues acting out his words

The interrogator leaned forward slightly so as to

make himself better heard by our guest, and he asked a single question. Then he simply left as briskly as he had arrived. He didn't even wait for an answer or any sort of reply, just left, *poof!*, as if he was never here.

Lad

Poof? Poof!? I can't believe my ears! As I lay sleeping, the interrogator enters our little box, stands behind our guest, asks a single question, and then departs, poof!, without waiting for an answer? Do you deceive me? Am I deceived?

Mate

I don't. You aren't. I have to admit, I found the whole thing a bit peculiar.

Lad

A bit peculiar? A bit peculiar? It's a bit peculiar to say the least, the very least, I should say. It might very well be the most peculiar thing I've heard of in this whole very peculiar war. And what, pray tell, did the interrogator ask our guest. I'm sure that his question will unravel this entire mysterious business. Well?

Mate

Well what?

Lad

What did the interrogator ask our guest? What was this one question that was so important that the interrogator made the journey here to ask, and yet so unimportant that he didn't bother to wait for an answer? What — I *implore* you! I *beseech* you! — what did the interrogator ask our guest?

Mate

Ah. He asked, "Why something instead of nothing?"

Lad

beat

What? No. What? Repeat the question. Say it again.

Mate

Why something instead of nothing?

Lad

*Lad slowly sinks to the floor in horror,
speaks in a frantic whisper*

No. It cannot be so. That cannot be the case. The interrogator could not have asked such a question. It is not to be believed. It is outside the bounds of reason. It is grotesquely, farcically, tragically absurd. What can it mean? What is the meaning of it? It defies reason! It is madness on top of madness. What does it mean?

Mate

Don't know. Haven't given it much thought.

Lad

Our guest speaks our tongue, then?

Mate

I don't know. He didn't speak.

Lad

But the interrogator must have thought he'd understand the question.

Mate

So it seems.

Lad

stands

So our guest has understood our every word?

Mate

Maybe so.

Lad

How can you be so calm? Why are you not in a panic?
Where is your rational madness?

Mate

You seem to have it managed.

Lad

Do I have this right? "Why something instead of nothing?" Was that the question?

Mate

It was. Exactly so.

Lad

Dear God.

spinning

I can feel my head unspooling on the vertical axis. I

am falling away in layers, peeling away in ribbons.

stops spinning

And how did our guest respond? Did he move? Did he make any gesture to indicate that he'd heard or understood?

Mate

Nothing.

Lad

And after? After the interrogator left? Has our guest made any motion since then?

Mate

No. Nothing.

Lad

My mind is a stomped watch.

stomping with both feet

Spring-sprang-sprung! Springy-sprangy-sprung! I feel as if my head will spin away in one direction and the earth in another. Such a question! Such a question! What do you make of it? What does the question mean?

Mate

Well, now that I've thought about it…

Lad

Yes, for chrissakes? Yes?

Mate

Don't know.

Lad

Lad falls to the floor, scrambles for his helmet and puts it on. He crawls to the near cot, turns it on its side and hides behind it. After a few beats he appears over the top edge, Kilroy-like.

We are at war! Men die in red waves! The earth burns and the skies are choked in blackness. Mothers lose their sons, girls their lads and babes their daddies. The world is mired in billowing gloom. Cannons and drums shake the mountains, nothing sparkles or shines, green and blue have been eradicated and nature herself is in exile. The final words are soon to be spoken, the light of the future sputters and dims, and now the interrogator, the one in whom our last sliver of hope resides, our one small chance to reverse the red tide and reclaim the garden, this man at long last makes his way to our mysterious guest, and what, for the love of all that is good and holy, what does the mighty interrogator ask? "Why something instead of nothing."

Mate

Yeah, that's it.

Lad

slamming the cot against the floor for

emphasis

Whadda ya mean, yeah that's it? Yeah that's what? That's not it, that's nothing! That's not a question! It makes no sense! It cannot be reconciled with our current circumstances! It does not make sense within the present context! You must have heard wrong!

Mate

Nope, clear as day. "Why something instead of nothing." More a statement than a question, really, or maybe the answer to a question we don't know.

Lad disappears down behind the cot
and reappears on the floor at the
downstage end of the cot. He crawls
to Mate's boot and wraps his arms
around it, beseeching.

Lad

It's not true, is it mate? Admit it, won't you? You're having a bit of sport with me, tell me you are. I understand, I really do. You find me tedious, my silly notions about peace and human values, I know it's all a bit storybook, I know I've been a bit of a boor going on about hopes and dreams and a life beyond war, a life of money-grubbing and child-rearing and frivolous frivolity; green grass and blue skies and laughing babies and all that fluff. I know I've been very foolish and I apologize to you, I really do, deeply, sincerely, bottom of my heart. But now please, *please* be kind and spring your little trap already. You've had your fun, you've had your little joke, and it was a good one! No denying that. I'm laughing, I know it's hard to see, but I am. *Ha ha! Ha ha!* I like a good joke mate, and I certainly had it coming...

Mate

stands and pronounces

All is vanity and a chasing after wind.

Lad

arms wrapped around Mate's leg

Is it? Yes, I suppose it is, vanity and wind chasing, I suppose it really is. But, you know, what the heck, right? What the heck, that's what I say. Vanity, wind, what the heck! I take your point, really I do. Now be a good man, be a good sport, and spare me, spare us all any further hijinks. Let us in on the joke, won't you mate?

Mate

steps forward, dragging boot-clutching Lad

Your question, it seems to me, is not whether I am having fun with you, which you know I am not, but rather, "Is it as it seems?" We say "It is what it is", but is it? Is it what it is? And the answer to that question is that no one can answer that question. No one, not the Lord God Almighty nor Lucifer, His Fallen Angel, nor Melba, Queen of All the Acrobats, can possibly know if what seems to be actually is what actually is. All, then – extending this simple and irrefutable observation to its admittedly disappointing conclusion – is vanity.

Lad

And a chasing after wind?

Mate

Yes, and a chasing after wind.

Lad

releases leg, crawls downstage center and kneels

Oh well, that certainly is disappointing, but also comforting in a way. I wish to continue pleading with you, but I've lost my vim. I wish to beat you to death, but I'm rather fond of you. I wish to blow my brains out, but I want to know what happens next. I wish to question the prisoner myself, but I'm afraid of what he'll say. I wish to march out onto the battlefield, but I don't want to be crushed beneath a stranger's boot. I wish to make a stand, but I think I should think about it some more.

folds hands in supplication, Mate approaches and stands beside Lad

I think I made a very bad mistake at some point, but I don't know what it was or how to fix it. I must have committed some terrible sin to end up here, some sin so great that it brought me to this end, but can you commit such a sin and not even know it? Can you arrive at such a place without knowing by what road you traveled?

Lad takes Mate's hand in both hands

It's you, isn't it mate? You're the interrogator, aren't you? You all along. It's okay mate, I understand, we all have our job to do. Is it you, mate? Are you he?

Mate

I've often asked myself that very question.

Lad

Ah well, it's all above my paygrade. Sorry I ate the entire saltine. What'll it be then? Rematch? Care to have another go at the Undisputed Pinky Touch Champion of the World?

Mate

I do.

Mate kneels down facing Lad in profile to audience and they resume their game.

lights fade

INTERMISSION 2

Girl

Yeah, me again... yeah, they do this gimmicky thing between acts so I just come out and call you...

looks in surprise at audience, speaks in audible whisper

Oh my God, I think these people are eavesdropping!

turns away, still audible

No, no more babies, but it's getting weird, I don't know... I guess it's just a bunch of different little skits, like, unrelated but kinda related, you know? Like, why not turn it into a story so people can understand it, right? Yeah, I know, right? Geez, don't make me work for it...

Guy

We still on for Sunday? Awesome. I don't know if she

likes sports, we only talked for a few minutes, had some appletinis first, you know... I think she's talking to her roommate... What? Yeah, I don't know, they just did this kinda creepy war thing, pretty wild but they're getting, I don't know, kinda philosophical or psychological or something... I don't know, I got the tickets for free... uh,

pats pockets

I don't know, play, I think, no, just play, play, supposed to be clever maybe...

Girl

Yeah, like torture, yeah! Like the last one was suicide and now it's torture... You think I should be worried about this guy? I know, right? What's the next one gonna be?

Guy

I don't know if I like it or not... you wanna just sit back and relax and this is like, you have to kinda think about it or something... yeah... like this one guy is all intense about patterns and he might be the guy they're waiting for but you're not sure, and the other guy is younger and he's worried about all the dams and planes and stuff, and there's a saltine, I guess you gotta see it... and there was this nurse, she was pretty good...

Girl

No, they didn't show any actual torture but I was really worried for this one guy, you could just tell he was gonna get it... you ever hear of pinky touch? like, a game?

laughs

Oh don't say that, the government's listening... Hey, you ever wonder why there's, like, something instead of nothing? Is that weird? That's a weird question, right? I know, but still, you know, it's kind of... oh, I know, next time I definitely pick, right? Yeah, if there is a... yeah, yeah, we'll see...

music begins

Guy

Okay, they're gonna get started again... next one's about a parade or something... yeah, really ... as long as it's not just a couple of old farts just *watching* a parade, right? Yeah, really... okay, later...

Act III: Parade

Transition music, sung by kids in a loop:

this is the song that never ends.
it just goes on and on my friends.
some people started singing it,
  not knowing what it was,
and they'll continue singing it forever
  just because...
this is the song that never ends.
it just goes on and on my friends...

SETTING

Along a small town parade route. Parade sounds such as drumming for marchers, music for band, etc, cheering of other spectators.

CHARACTERS

Husband & Wife: They are nearly identical; pale, chubby, seventy-ish. Large straw sunhats, flip-up sunglasses, white sunblock on noses, untucked Hawaiian shirts, knee-length khaki shorts, socks, sandals. They sit in cheap aluminum folding chairs. Both have small flags that they sometimes wave or gesture with. He has a folded up newspaper. She has a purse and her knitting. Both address each other directly and audience aside.

> *A Sousa-type march plays as Husband waves flag and Wife applauds with bouncy, seal-like enthusiasm. They are obviously watching a parade. Husband lays a hand on Wife's forearm to slow her clapping. The music fades.*

Husband

Please stop that, dear.

Wife

What? I'm only clapping. That's what you're supposed to do at a parade, dear.

Husband

Save something for the clowns.

Wife

Silly old poop!

> *slaps Husband's forearm playfully*

Mister Stick-in-the-Butt. Never let a girl have a nice time!

Husband

Stick in the *mud*, dear, not stick in the *butt*.

Wife

Same thing.

Husband

Very different.

Wife

Oh, I love a parade. It's so exciting! Oooh, it's giving me the bubbles.

taps his forearm

You hear that, dear? I'm getting the bubbles!

Husband

Yes dear, I heard you.

Husband Aside

The problem is, she uses the word bubbles to mean two different physiological events, two very different physiological events, and you guess wrong at your peril.

Wife Aside

You wouldn't know it from looking at him, but he's not a bad man. Good husband, good provider, good father and grandfather, what more can you ask?

Husband

What's that, dear?

Wife

I said, this is a nice spot, isn't it dear?

Husband

Oh yes, very nice spot, dear.

Wife

Are you savoring the moment, dear?

Husband

leans in

What's that, dear?

Wife

Savoring the moment, dear. I asked if you're savoring the moment.

Husband

Well, no dear, not right now I'm not.

Wife

If not now, when? If not here, where? Try to make an effort, dear, it's important.

Husband

Yes, dear.

Wife Aside

I have to remind him to savor or he'll just grumble. I think it's much nicer to savor than grumble.

Wife

Do you think there'll be elephants, dear?

Husband

None for the last fifty-two years, dear, probably none today.

Wife

Fifty-two years, my, my. How many parades have we been to, do you think?

Husband

You and me?

Wife

Yes dear, you and me.

Husband

Ever?

Wife

Yes dear, ever.

Husband

I don't know, dear.

counts on fingers

Memorial Day, Veterans Day, Homecoming, Thanksgiving, Easter, Saint Pat's, fifty some-odd years, four hundred parades, I guess.

Wife Aside

Or, as he's about to tell you, one parade four hundred times.

Husband Aside

In truth we've been to one parade four hundred times; this parade, always the same. Me and the wife have been to this exact same parade four hundred times.

Wife Aside

He thinks I don't know what he thinks, but grumbly people think grumbly thoughts. He thinks himself a man of many profound philosophical insights, but he got them all from t-shirts and bumper stickers.

Husband Aside

She thinks I'm her nice sweet man. She has no idea I have thoughts of my own, thoughts I don't share. Look at this newspaper, for instance. I've read this exact same newspaper twenty-thousand times. Every day of my adult life I have read this exact same newspaper. There is nothing new...

band music interrupts

Wife

Oh look, dear! It's the high school band!

Husband

Yes, dear.

both plug their ears and scrunch their faces as music gets louder and eventually passes

Wife

Wasn't that nice?

Husband

snapping fingers next to ears

Very nice, dear.

Wife

rummaging through purse

Would you like a nice piece of licorice, dear? I brought some nice licorice.

Husband

Do you have any crack cocaine in there, dear? I've been thinking about taking it up. Heard a lotta good things. Or maybe some nice angel dust? It's all the rage.

Wife

Angel dust? Oh my, doesn't that sound heavenly.

rummaging in purse

Um, no, no, I don't think I have any angel dust, but I have a nice licorice somewhere.

Wife Aside

Our grandkids are going to have kids of their own, soon. Can you imagine? Me and Mr. Sour-Puss over here are going to be great-grammy and great-grampy. He pretends he's not excited but I know he is.

Husband Aside

The problem with life is it's too damn long. What are you supposed to do with all this time? Thirty-six, forty years, that's a good lifespan. Get in, get married, raise some kids, and get out. That makes sense. This hanging around for decades makes no sense at all. There is nothing new. There is nothing new under the...

Wife

Oh look dear, here come the majorettes twirling their batons!

Wife Aside

And now we get to hear about 1962...

Husband

Get ready to duck! You remember that time in 1962 when one of them batons come flying straight at my head? Right past my ear! Could've killed me. And that little girl with the braces ran over to pick it up and she didn't even say sorry for nearly knocking my head off...

Wife Aside

knitting, Husband still speaking in background

You'd think at some point I'd throw a hairdryer in his bath just to shut him up, but I actually find it very comforting. He doesn't seem to have a memory in the usual sense, so every time he says something he thinks it's new and interesting. I've heard it all a million times, so I know the right places to nod or chuckle or say "oh my" without having to listen, and that's how we get along after all these years.

Husband

regaining volume, Wife feigning interest

...lucky I didn't sue. People should be issued helmets if they're going to let little girls hurl deadly weapons into the crowd.

Husband Aside

Have I told that one before? Or course I have. I know it. Did it really happen? Doesn't matter. I have a head full of stories and opinions and snappy comebacks, all just waiting for the right button to be pressed. That's all it takes. Some word or event hits a play button in my head and the correct response comes out – familiar, well-practiced, smooth as silk – an actor playing a role. Hold on.

Husband

*taps wife's leg with newspaper and
points audience left*

Look dear, here come the businessmen on tricycles.

Wife

Oh, bubbles! Bubbles! Maybe they'll throw us a candy!

Husband Aside

Nobody dreams of such a life, you just wake up one day and find yourself in it. You're not a ballplayer or a cop or a hitman and you never will be. It starts before you even know the other thing has ended. It starts as soon as you get on the right track. As soon as you get on the right track, it's over. If I could go back now and have a talk with myself as a young man, that would be my advice; do not get on the right track. The right track is *not* the right track, it's a rut, and once you fall in you never get out. Now she'll offer sunblock for my nose.

Wife

Would you like some sunblock for your nose, dear?

Husband

No thank you, dear. I still have some on.

Husband Aside

There's a decisive moment early in life, but it's not clearly marked, and if you're not paying attention you go zipping right past it, and then it's gone and you don't know you missed it until fifty years later when you're waving your little flag and watching the parade go by.

Wife Aside

The poor man can't find pleasure in the little things. Savor, I tell him, savor! This parade may be your last.

Husband Aside

Is today the day I finally tear off my clothes and smear myself in excrement and join the parade twirling my own baton? That would get their attention. Then they'd take notice. Never mind that I have a distinguished war record or that I did my job for five decades or that I provided for my family and never complained. That's not enough anymore. These days, if you want to make your mark, a mark that won't disappear the day they stick you in the ground, you have to get off the right track and make a mess. Marching in the big parade naked and smeared in feces may not be heroic, but it would make a mark!

Wife Aside

I know he struggles with his lot in life – *coulda been somebody! coulda been a contenduh!* – he doesn't understand the difference between playing a role and performing a function. Everyone wants to be the star of the show, everyone wants to be the hero, but if we're all heroes, then who sits on the sidewalk and claps? It's natural to dream of being up on stage slaying the dragon and saving the princess, but what could be nicer than watching from the audience? You get to let someone else deal with all the muss and fuss, and then you get to go back to your nice little box and savor.

Husband Aside

stands and orates

What do people gain from all their labors? Generations come and generations go, the sun rises and sets, the wind blows, rivers flow into the sea. Is there anything one can point to...

points dramatically

...and say, "Look! This is something new"? What *is* has been before and will be again. What is *done* has been done before and will be done again. I have seen much of wisdom and knowledge, and also madness and folly, and I learned that this, too, is a chasing after wind. There is nothing new... there is nothing new...

under the sun!

    sits

Wife Aside

  singsong

And many words mark the speech of a fool.

Husband

taps Wife's leg with newspaper

You know what I sometimes think, dear?

Wife

waving her flag

That you haven't made your mark, dear? That you missed the decisive moment? That your life has somehow passed you by?

Husband

Well, uh...

Wife

That if you had it to do all over again, you'd do it differently? That youth is wasted on the young and that your many years have taught you a thing or two?

Husband

I mean, well, uh, yeah...

Wife

wife stands, faces audience, oration
building

That it's too late now? That your great symphony will go unwritten? That you will leave no sign of having passed this way?

in full preacher mode now, pointing
with flag

That you hear the blacksmith at his anvil and the sawyer at his boards as you stand upon the tailor's pedestal? Stand up! Arise!

Husband

What?

Wife

Get up!

Husband

stands, faces wife timidly

Well, okay, I guess...

Wife

as if possessed

And the tailor of men asks of thee, "Which way does the gentleman dress?"

Husband

What now? Excuse me?

Wife

"Which way?" asks the tailor. "Which way does the gentleman dress?"

Husband

Dress? Oh, uh...

turns away from wife, looks down to check

...uh, left, I guess. Left.

Wife

And does the gentleman suppose the gentleman can dress *right* simply because the gentleman might have a notion to do so?

Husband

Um, well, no, I can't just...

floppy left-to-right gesture

Wife

No indeed! The gentleman dresses left and that's the way of it. One cannot just *swiiing* oneself over...

gesturing side to side with flag

...from left to right or right to left, can one? One is endowed as one is endowed, is one not? What would the world be if all the gentlemen dressed other than as endowed?

Husband

If who did what now?

Wife

If all the gentlemen dressed other than as endowed, then the natural order would be violated. Violated in principle! Violated in essence! A false note sounds. World on fire. The misalignment of the gentlemen heralds the misalignment of the cosmos. Fabric wrinkled. Unsightly bulges. Chaffing. End of days.

Husband

End of days? Just because I switch my...?

Wife

Pattern itself would be disrupted! And does the gentleman know what – above all else! – does the gentleman know what cannot possibly happen? What can never, ever possibly happen?

Husband

Uh, no... what?

Wife

Wife sits and becomes herself again

Pattern cannot be disrupted, dear. Not possible. Pattern can never possibly be disrupted. Just can't happen.

she pats his chair, he sits, stunned

The disruption simply becomes the pattern, you see. Isn't that clever? Now be a lamb and have a nice licorice and savor the moment.

hands him a licorice

Here's a clean one. Savor that. There's my big fella. Are you savoring?

Husband

Yes dear, I'm savoring.

taps Wife's leg with newspaper and points audience left

Look, dear, here come the clowns.

Wife

Oooh, bubbles! Bubbles! Maybe they'll throw us a candy!

lights fade

Intermission 3

Guy

Oh my God! It *was* just a couple of old farts watching a parade! I know, like I'm psychic or something, right? ... Hey, when a tailor asks you which way you dress? ... yeah, okay okay... don't say that, the government's listening... yeah, that's what I thought... no, there's no tailor... well, the old lady was kinda possessed by a tailor I guess... no, no, I don't know...

Girl

Oh my God! Why did he bring me to this? I know, right? You think he wants me to think he's smart or something? When he said a play I thought there'd be a lot of, you know, wherefore art thous and stuff, but this is more like, hey, I'm gonna take my clothes off and smear myself in poo and twirl my baton and stuff... I know, an old guy, right? No, he didn't really do it...

Guy

Yeah, I think she's enjoying it...

they share a wave

It's a little awkward cause you're not always sure when to laugh... like this old lady gets these bubbles and you're, like, is that kinda funny or kinda gross or what. Yeah, next time I'll just take her to a game so you always know when to cheer and when to boo, forget all this culture crap...

Girl

He put his hand on my hand, it was so awkward, like high school or something... I know, right? You don't want to pull away but where do the hands go? I know, man up buddy, right? Don't be such a... yeah, I know, I know... Yeah, he's on the phone right now, probably telling his friends he's gonna score tonight... I know, right? Not unless this play starts getting its act together... Ooh, I just made a pun! I didn't know I could do that! I should write that down...

Guy

I don't know... she likes appletinis, yeah, like eleven bucks a pop, yeah, so, we'll probably do that and see... yeah, I got an early thing ... yeah, hey, you ever think about patterns? No, I don't know, just how, like, everything might be part of, you know, like some larger thing, like there's just this one big...

music begins

Oh, hold on, they're gonna start up again. They start each thing with a nursery rhyme, I wonder how many of these things there are... I don't know, I don't know, something about a debate...

Act IV: Debate

Transition music sung by children:

> *humpty dumpty sat on a wall,*
> *humpty dumpty had a great fall.*
> *all the king's horses and all the king's men*
> *couldn't put humpty together again.*

> *repeat*

CHARACTERS & SETTING

MODERATOR: Thirty-something female
SCIENCE: Stately male in labcoat
RELIGION: Stately male in priest garb
PHILOSOPHY: 15 year-old female

Scene opens on a stage like any informal debate. A handmade sign on an easel reads:

Tonight's Topic: The Nature of Reality

Three lecterns with microphones, water bottles, etc. PHILOSOPHY middle, RELIGION and SCIENCE left and right. To the side sits MODERATOR at a desk with microphone, water, clipboard.

Moderator

Welcome to tonight's debate on the nature of reality. Viewpoints being represented tonight will be Religion, Philosophy and Science. I'll push through the introductions so we can get right to it.

consulting clipboard

Representing religion is His Eminence Bishop Anthony Dellacroce, doctor of divinity and chairman of the university's religious studies department.

hearty applause from audience

Representing the scientific point of view is Dr. Lionel Gelding, astrophysicist and quantum physicist and chair of the applied sciences department.

hearty applause from audience

And representing philosophy this evening will be Dr. Stanislav Paradovsky, holder of multiple degrees in various philosophical disciplines and professor emeritus...

Philosophy

Uh, hello? Excuse me?

Moderator

One moment, sir. Dr. Paradovsky is also a devoted

husband, father of four and grandfather of seven. Dr. Paradovsky, did you wish to comment?

Philosophy

Uh, yeah, like uh, I'm not him.

Moderator

You're, like uh, not who, Dr. Paradovsky?

Philosophy

Yes.

Moderator

Yes what?

Philosophy

I'm not Dr. Paradovsky.

Moderator

Ah. And why not?

Philosophy

Dr. Paradovsky gave me his invitation and told me to...

Moderator

I don't understand. Are you a member of the philosophy department?

Philosophy

No, actually, I'm a sophomore in high school. I just had some questions about some, uh, you know, stuff, so I went to see Dr. Paradovsky and he...

Moderator

You're in the tenth grade?

Philosophy

brisk cadence, youthful lilt

Well, yeah, uh… so I read this thing by Plato, the philosopher guy, and he said, like, how can we know if we're really standing here talking, or if we're actually asleep and just dreaming the whole thing, so that got me thinking, and the more I thought about it the more I wasn't sure. So then I asked my homeroom teacher some questions that I thought were pretty simple, but she called me a smartass and said I should go to the university with my questions. So I did! I went to the philosophy department and I was following Dr. Paradovsky around asking my questions, but I don't think he wanted to talk to me. And then his secretary reminded him that he had this debate on his schedule so he handed me his invitation and told me to go. He said I was a very annoying child and that this was the right place for me. I thought I'd just be in the audience, but when they saw the invitation they put me up here.

Moderator

Well, this is highly irregular, but uh… what's your name?

Philosophy

Penny DeWitt.

Moderator

looks off to the wings for a ruling,
finally shrugs

Well, okay then. As a designated representative of Professor Paradovsky; Penny DeWitt.

weak applause

Science

Excuse me? You're going to let a high school kid participate in a sanctioned debate with department heads from respected institutions?

Moderator

That's correct.

Religion

It's absurd! Paradovsky can't send someone to represent him just because he finds them annoying.

Moderator

It's a debate format, gentlemen. If you defeat her arguments then there shouldn't be a problem.

Philosophy

Uh, hello? Hi, I don't really have any arguments.

Moderator

There, see? Easy peasy, hope to die. Moving on. For purposes of clarity, our three participants will be referred to by their respective fields; Religion, Philosophy and Science. Any questions? Okay, let's

begin. Religion, in one brief sentence, please summa-
rize your view of whiffleball.

Religion

Whiffleball?

Moderator

checks clipboard

Reality.

Religion

The reality is that God is the uncreated creator of the
universe and we are his children.

Moderator

Science, same question.

Science

The reality is that the universe is governed by immu-
table laws, and by observation and the application of
scientific methodology we can come to understand
what those laws are.

Moderator

Thank you. Philosophy?

Philosophy

What?

Moderator

What is your summary statement? What view of reality will you be defending tonight?

Philosophy

Oh, I don't have one. That's why I was following Dr. Paradovsky around. I just wanted to ask some questions and he called me a little brat and, you know, sent me here.

Moderator

Are you sure you wish to continue with this?

Philosophy

Well, yeah. Like I said, I just had some questions, like, uh, why is there something instead of nothing? I mean, that seems like kind of an obvious thing, but...

Moderator

Okay, Religion, why is there something instead of nothing?

Religion

Because of God.

aside

Duh!

Moderator

Science? Why is there something instead of nothing?

Science

How could there be nothing? It doesn't make any sense. Reality isn't nothing, it's something.

aside

Duh!

Philosophy

Yeah, but is reality real?

Moderator

Okay, Science, is reality real?

Science

Seems pretty real to me.

Moderator

Religion, is reality real?

Religion

I don't understand. What else would it be?

Moderator

Okay. Philosophy?

Philosophy

But how do we know? How do I know I'm even awake? How do we know anything?

Moderator

Okey-doke. Religion, how do we know anything?

Religion

We are informed by the Holy Spirit and illuminated by the spark of the divine.

Philosophy

Yeah, but wait a minute...

Moderator

Wait your turn. Science? How do we know anything?

Science

We arrive at knowledge through rigorous observation, measurement and testing, through studies and reproducible experiments, and through the process of publishing and peer review.

Philosophy

Um, excuse me? I don't think you understood the question... I don't mean why do we *believe*, I mean how do we *know*?

Religion

When you open your heart to the love of Christ...

Science

Oh, for the love of Christ! Experiment, measurement, review. That's how we know.

Moderator

Philosophy, same question. How do we know anything?

Philosophy

I don't know, that's why I asked. I mean, I know I exist because I can't be wrong about that, but I can be wrong about everything else, right?

Religion

tiredly

Young lady, there is nothing new or exciting about your solipsistic approach.

Science

condescendingly

We are all quite familiar with the Cartesian idea that the universe can't be known to exist, and I assure you, we have left this little conundrum behind long ago.

Philosophy
Awesome! That's great, that's why I'm here. How? How did you get past this problem?

Science
Oh, well, we uh… we just scooted right past it.

Religion
Danced right around it.

Science
Gave it a wide berth.

Religion
Steered well clear.

Science
Turned a blind eye.

Religion
A deaf ear.

Science
Left it behind…

Religion
…and never looked back.

Philosophy

Oh. Maybe I don't understand. If you could just let me know how you solved the problem of how we can be sure of anything, then I can go home. That's really all I came for.

Science

I can assure you, young lady – and I speak for the entire scientific community when I say this – everything is exactly as it seems.

Religion

Yes, young lady. Science and religion may not agree about much, but we certainly agree about this. The way things seem is the way things are. In short, it is what it is.

Philosophy

Is it?

Science

It is, and now that you have what you came for, goodbye.

Religion

Off with you. Begone!

Philosophy

Okay, thank you, I'll go now. But... excuse me, what was it again? I'm sorry, I should have written it down. How do we know anything? How do I know I'm not just dreaming or living in a computer simulation? How do I know that what I call reality is not just a multi-sensory projection in the theater of my mind?

Science
Objection!

Moderator
This is not a trial. What's your objection?

Science
Asked and answered!

Religion
Argumentative!

Science
Badgering!

Religion
I want her comments stricken from the record.

Moderator
No record, not a trial. Please state your specific objection.

Science
Well, for one thing, it's dumb. How's that?

Moderator
Not very good.

Religion
She hasn't even taken a basic philosophy course, so she doesn't know how this issue has been resolved.

Moderator
And now she's asking. She asked her teachers and

they wouldn't answer. Then she went to the university and they wouldn't answer. And now she's here. Will you answer? How has the issue of the impossibility of objective knowledge been resolved?

Religion

Well, as it happens, it hasn't...

Science

Yes, there seems to be a minor technicality...

Moderator

Well, then the question seems to be whether or not science has any basis in fact.

Science

What, are you nuts? It's *all* facts! That's what science is, facts! Here,

slaps hand on podium

this podium is a fact!

holds up hand

This hand is a fact! This air, this light, the eyes with which we see, the ears with which we hear, all facts!

Religion

Facts require proof. Have you any proof?

Science

Christ, who's side are you on?

Religion

Christ's.

Moderator

Science? Response?

Science

To what?

Moderator

You seem to be saying that everything is just as it seems. Can you prove that? Can you prove, well, *anything?*

Science

What do you mean, prove? It's obvious!

Moderator

It actually doesn't seem that obvious. Can either of you please answer Miss DeWitt's question? It's a very reasonable question and she has been very polite. You two gentlemen are experts in your fields so you must have some knowledge you can share. Religion, you first, how do you know you're not just dreaming everything?

Religion

Man has present within him the spark of the divine, and as we contain within us that which is of God, so we contain within us that which is all-knowing.

Philosophy

But how do you know God's not dreaming everything?

Religion

Because then he wouldn't be God, he'd be a loony-bird.

Moderator

So the question is, does God have knowledge?

Religion

Of course God has knowledge! He's God, for chrissakes! He knows everything!

Philosophy

But how do you *know* He knows?

Religion

Because the Bible tells me so!

Philosophy

But how do you know the Bible is right?

Religion

frantic

Because it's the word of God!

Science

Oh my God, would you please leave the poor man alone. Can't you see his entire position is solid as a snot bubble?

Moderator

Okay then Science, would you please answer the young lady's question so we can move on?

Science

Certainly. Anything to get this debate back on the right track. What was the question again?

Moderator

Philosophy, please restate your question.

Philosophy

You can *believe* anything, but to *know* something it has to be true. You can't know something that isn't true, so only truth can be known.

waves to indicate surroundings

This could all be a dream or a computer simulation or anything else, so my question is; How do I know anything? For instance, I see this podium and I see all you people who seem to see this podium, therefore, I *believe* the podium exists, but can I ever *know* this podium exists?

Science

Of course you can know the podium exists!

Philosophy

Awesome! How?

Science

It's apparent! It's right there! How can you say it's not? You're looking right at it. Your hands are on it. You see it, you feel it, you can smell it, you can knock on it and listen to it. You can stick out your little tongue and...

Moderator

Okay. Philosophy, how do you respond?

Philosophy

To what?

Moderator

Science's response.

Philosophy

But he didn't say how I know, he said why I should believe. I know appearances are very convincing, but my senses can deceive me. What I want to know is how I *know*. How do I know any of this is real?

Science

Young lady, if you were an actual philosopher, you would know that there is no such thing as objectively true knowledge, only justified subjective belief.

Religion

Justified subjective belief? Point of order! If science can't prove anything, then it's a belief system.

Science

Science is not a belief system! Science is... *science!*

Religion

What's wrong with being a belief system? After all our bickering... Embrace me brother!

Science

Ack!

Religion

Let the record show that Science just admitted that it is, indeed, a belief system.

Science

A *justified* belief system.

Religion

It is only justified by consensus. Other people validate you, but who validates them?

Science

Are you suggesting that the audience doesn't exist?

Religion

Can you prove they do? Can you prove *you* do?

Science

Are you suggesting... wait, what *are* you suggesting?

Religion

I'm saying I believe the audience exists.

Science

Well, I don't believe in belief.

Religion

There's only knowledge and belief. It must be one or the other, so what do you believe?

Science

I believe in facts!

Religion

Which is a belief.

Science

Facts are facts, not beliefs.

Religion

So you believe.

Science

Facts are not beliefs!

Religion

So you believe.

Science

Facts don't require belief!

Religion

So you believe.

Science

So I know!

Religion

Believing doesn't make it so.

Science

That's rich coming from you! As soon as science solves the problem of death, all your churches will turn to burger joints.

Religion

And as soon as the Son of Man returns, all your laboratories will turn to lavatories.

Science

What is crooked cannot be straightened!

Religion

What is lacking cannot be counted!

Moderator

gavels with hand on desk

Order! Order in the friendly debate! Please, gentlemen, stop your senseless bickering.

Religion

But that's what we do.

Science

Yeah, it's kind of our thing.

Religion

That's why they keep having us back.

Science

Even though nothing ever gets settled.

Religion

Because nothing ever gets settled.

Science

And that's why we don't like to invite philosophy to
our debates. They always muck it up with all their
logic and reason.

Religion

Yeah, look at the mess this little girl has made with
one simple question!

*approaches Philo and stands to one
side of her podium*

Look kid, we got a good thing here, okay? Look out
there,

indicates audience

you see anybody asking you to come here tonight
and rock the boat?

Science

*approaches Philo and stands on the
other side of her podium*

Why rock the boat? We have a two-party system
and everyone's happy with that. The brain has two
hemispheres, see? There's no third half, that's just
basic math, right?

Religion

It's basic math. The church is thousands of years old.
Millions of devoted followers, beautiful buildings,
lovely attire. What are you? You're just some kid.

Science

Just some kid. Do you really presume to stand here
and argue with the likes of Newton and Einstein and
Hawking?

Religion

God loves you, honey. Don't you want to love him
back?

Science

Science is all about facts, kiddo. You like facts, don't
you?

Religion

You want to go to heaven someday, don't you?

                    Science

Or outer space?

                    Religion

You don't want to go to hell, do you?

                    Science

Or die of cancer?

                    Religion

Philosophy can't produce miracles.

                    Science

Or create vaccines.

                    Religion

Or grant sainthood.

                    Science

Or feed the world.

                    Religion

Or forgive your sins.

                    Science

Or make the fun ones safer.

                    Religion

They don't put philosophy books in hotel rooms, do they?

                    Science

They don't ask philosophy to split the atom, do they?

Religion

You're not going to have a philosopher perform your wedding, are you?

Science

Or your baby's baptism?

Religion

Or your parents' funerals?

Science

Has philosophy put a man on the moon?

Religion

Built any great cathedrals?

Science

Cured any disease?

Religion

Caused any wars?

Science

Won any wars?

Religion

in a high, mocking voice

Oh hi! I'm philosophy! I think, therefore I am!

Science

in a high, mocking voice

Yeah! I like to wear sandals and think all day!

BOTH

La-di-da-la-di-da...

Moderator

Gentlemen...

Science

Can philosophy do this?

makes a funny face

Religion

Or this?

does a funny dance

Science

No! Philosophy just sits there.

Religion

Like a lump.

Science

A lumpy little lump!

Moderator

gavels with hand on desk

Order in the debate! Gentlemen! Please! Back to your podiums!

they return

Moderator

If there is a record, that last exchange will be stricken. If there is a jury, they are instructed to ignore it. Let me remind everyone that Philosophy has asked one simple question; How do we know anything? It seems like a very reasonable question and so far she has received no answer.

Religion

dabbing his brow

Simple questions can be the hardest. I know that God is a living presence in all our lives, but I certainly can't prove it.

Science

fixing his hair

We can calculate pi to a billion digits, but we can't prove that a circle exists. We can trace creation back to the big bang, but we can't prove that the universe exists.

Religion

See what philosophy does?

Science

Philosophy is dead.

Religion

Philosophy is dead!

Science

Modern philosophy represents little more than the failure of college counselors to guide incoming freshmen away from the hollow trappings of intellectual vanity.

Religion

All is vanity!

Science

And a chasing after...

Philosophy

Wait! I'm not a philosopher! I'm just asking a question.

Religion

According to you, you're the only one in the whole universe and the rest of us are just characters in your dream!

Philosophy

I never said that! Just because I know what's *not* true doesn't mean I know what *is*, and not knowing what *is* true doesn't mean I don't know what's *not*.

Religion

Ah, from the mouths of babes.

Philosophy

flattered

Oh, hey, thanks.

Moderator

Philosophy, you were saying?

Philosophy

Well, I'm not saying you're all characters in my dream, I'm just asking how I can be sure. I mean, that's pretty obvious, right? I know that everybody believes everything is just as it seems, but truth isn't a popularity contest. And in response to the comment by science, I guess I pretty much agree.

Science

What? No, wait... what? I object! I don't want to be agreed with. This is a debate, is she allowed to agree with me?

Moderator

I'll allow it. Philosophy, what in particular are you agreeing with?

Philosophy

That philosophy is dead.

Religion

Good. Then it's settled. This debate should be limited to science and religion. She admits philosophy is dead, so why do we need her?

Moderator

Philosophy was invited, just like you.

Religion

But she just said philosophy is dead!

Philosophy

Can I say something?

Moderator

Go on, sweetie.

Philosophy

The reason I agree that philosophy is dead is because it lacks a solid foundation, and since religion and science both depend on the same false foundation as philosophy...

Science

Objection!

Religion

Sustained!

Moderator

It's not a trial.

Philosophy

Well, maybe it should be a trial. Let's put reality on trial. Religion has their version, Science has their version, and my only version is how do I know I'm not dreaming? Or plugged into a computer? Or something else? How do I know any of this is real? How do I even know if there is a universe? How do I know anything?

Religion

Objection!

Science

Sustained!

Moderator

Not a trial.

Religion

Why is she even here? She's just a kid!

Science

No wonder Paradovsky gave her the boot.

Moderator

Rules, please. Philosophy, would you like to further address the points raised by Science?

Philosophy

Science and religion are based on the theory that everything is as it seems, but is it? That's a fair question, isn't it? We say "it is what it is", but is it?

Religion

Is what it?

Science

Is what what?

Philosophy

Is it what it is? Is it as it seems?

Science

It's indisputable!

Philosophy

We're disputing it right now.

Religion

It's self-evident!

Philosophy

Only self is self-evident.

Science

Objection!

Moderator

It's not a… oh, fine. On what grounds?

Science

Badgering respectable people!

Religion

Badgering the clergy!

Moderator

Overruled.

Science

I declare a mistrial!

Moderator

Dream on.

Philosophy

You two aren't here to debate, you're just here to bicker. You're like an old married couple, the left-brained husband and his right-brained wife. That's why you don't like Philosophy at your debates. Philosophy relies on logic and reason, which is like Kryptonite to you people.

Science
You try defending consensus reality as if it were real.

Religion
It's exhausting.

Philosophy
What's consensus reality?

Moderator
It means reality is as we all agree it is rather than as we know it is.

Philosophy
So then, science is consensus science?

Science
No!

Religion
Obviously.

Philosophy
And religion is consensus religion?

Religion
No!

Science
Obviously.

Religion
Consensus reality is like paper money. It has no value except everyone believes in it. It has no real value, only pretend value, which is fine as long as everyone

keeps pretending.

Science
Now we are confronted with a young girl who will not pretend, who has pointed at the emperor in his new clothes and declared him naked.

Religion
When the world is a lie, to doubt is heresy.

Science
And the raiser of doubt a heretic.

Philosophy
What's a heretic?

Science
A bull in a china shop.

Philosophy
But I'm just asking questions.

Religion
That's all it takes.

Philosophy
I came here tonight all excited thinking "Oh boy! Now the real experts will answer my questions!" But there are no real experts, are there?

Science
Objection! Argumentative.

Philosophy
It's a debate!

Religion

Ambiguous!

Philosophy

It's black and white.

Science

Calls for speculation!

Philosophy

It calls for an answer.

Religion

Calls for conclusion!

Philosophy

Yes! Exactly! What's wrong with that?

Science

Objection!

Moderator

On what grounds?

Science

Improper credentials!

Religion

Lack of decorum!

Science

Disruptive influence!

Religion

Violation of protocol!

Science

Extremely annoying!

Philosophy

I object to you, how's that? Both of you! Lack of foundation, that's a real one, isn't it? Beyond the scope of the witness, how's that for an objection? Assumes facts not in evidence, how do you like that one?

> *Science and Religion both have their*
> *eyes shut and their fingers stuck in*
> *their ears, and they're making gibber-*
> *ish sounds so they can't hear anything.*

And Philosophy is no better from what I can tell.

> *Religion and Science stop their noise-*
> *making and listen.*

Philosophy is dead, and I think that's because, if you think about it, there's really nothing to think about. I think I am so I know I am, and everything else is just a crapshoot. Objective knowledge is impossible. There, I said it! What's so hard about that? What's everyone so afraid of?

Science

You presume to tell us what's true?

Philosophy

I presume to ask.

Religion

Well, we didn't come to answer.

Science

We came to debate!

Religion

I rest my case.

Science

Case closed.

Moderator

rises and leans on front of desk

Well, Penny DeWitt, it looks like your answer is no answer. There is no such thing as objective knowledge. Truth and knowledge are things we can profess but never possess, so we live in a world of make-believe and make believe we don't. Are you satisfied with that?

Philosophy

Yes, because it's true.

Moderator

Closing comments. Science?

Science

It's true that truth is not a standard to which science can be held. Yes, I admit it; even though I stand here in the light, I cannot prove that light exists, or time or space, or even matter for that matter. But truth is not the job of science. The job of science is to deal with what we can as well as we can and to build upon it to carry us all into the future.

exits

Moderator

Closing comments. Religion?

Religion

Nothing said here today alters my views in the least. If anything, we have only deepened my certainty in the love and goodness of God. Religion is the heartfelt and indwelling gift of faith, and no claim of science or cleverness of philosophy could ever extinguish in me that which illuminates my innermost being. Religion is the guiding light of billions of lives and the darker life gets the brighter faith burns. Thank you for your presence here tonight, Miss DeWitt. I hope you find, if not answers, at least peace.

exits

Moderator

Closing comments. Philosophy?

Philosophy

It is what it is, they say, but is it? Does anything really exist? Is there something? Does nothing exist? Is zero a number? Am I a butterfly dreaming I'm a girl falling into a rabbit hole? I'll never know, but now I know that I'll never know, and maybe knowing that I know nothing is something.

exits

Moderator

slams hand on desk

Debate adjourned!

lights fade

Intermission 4

Girl

I can't talk long, I gotta pee... it's okay, I'm sure the government knows people gotta pee... no, no, yeah, it was like a debate thing, I wonder how many more of these things there are... I don't know, these old guys were kinda picking on this girl and she kinda kicked their butts, but then it ended nice... it was funny, a lot of back and forth stuff... I don't know, they're asking these big life questions or something... I know, who's got time, right?

Guy

Man, okay, that was kinda weird... they had this little girl and she was kinda stuck in a debate, right? And she was like, asking these really simple questions, I mean, you know, obvious stuff, and these like really smart old guys, like a religious guy and a science guy, and they just couldn't deal, right? And the kid, the girl, you know, she wasn't real smart or anything, but...

you know, like, the emperor's new clothes? ... Yeah, it was like that, like this kid just saw through all their pompous bullsh... what? yeah, I don't know though, I might have to google some of this stuff later, maybe read a book...

Girl

Yeah, who knows? He probably got the tickets free or something... you know you can't even have snacks? I know, what a gyp! You just gotta sit there and watch... I was kinda nodding off but then they kept slapping their hands on the desks and stuff and I'm like okay, I'm awake! ... You know, science does all sorts of cool stuff, right? I mean, you can't really make fun of science, can you? They know what they're doing, right? ... I know, right? But did you ever kinda wonder... no, it's dumb... no, never mind...

music begins

Gotta go. Yeah, no, no, I don't know... I don't know... I don't know... yeah, I'll hang a sock on the door... yeah, okay... later...

Act V: Anatta

Transition music, sung by kids:

while the moon her watch is keeping
all through the night
while the weary world is sleeping
all through the night
o'er thy spirit gently stealing
visions of delight revealing
breathes a pure and holy feeling
all through the night

SETTING

Semi-rustic cabin interior, messy, lived in. The space is softly lit with candles and lamps. Entry door and stone fireplace audience left where a fire burns. Rocking chair beside the fireplace and a couch facing it. Audience right, kitchenette, hall and bathroom out of view. Nearby a telephone stand with an old black rotary phone and a wall mirror. Downstage audience right, a small dining table used as a messy desk, littered with paper in sheets and crumpled balls, water bottles, coffee cups, etc, a laptop on one end and a printer on a chair, a desk lamp lights the laptop and more debris. A waste basket is overflowing and surrounded by crumpled paper.

CHARACTER

Julie: Thirty-ish female. Frazzled, haggard, possibly insane. Thin. Wears loose jeans and a baggy sweater, unkempt, no make-up, bare feet. Long messy hair.

> *As lights come up we hear sounds*
> *of groans and retching. JULIE enters*
> *from bathroom, shutting off light and*
> *fan, wiping mouth on a face towel.*
> *She looks haggard, wipes mouth,*
> *tosses towel on floor, disappears into*
> *kitchenette. We hear fridge open and*
> *shut, bottle opening, gargling and*
> *spitting. She emerges with a plastic*
> *water bottle. She drinks some and sets*
> *it down among others littered about.*
> *She picks up a pad of paper and a*
> *pen from table and paces downstage*
> *center and scribbles almost violently*
> *before tearing the page off and throw-*
> *ing it aside.*

JULIE

No, no, no! C'mon godammit! Stop it, stop! Stop

talking bullshit. Stop trying to go around it! Say it right! Stop trying to squirm away from it like such a...

she stops pacing, writes manically, tears the sheet loose and throws it aside, starts again

No, no, what's wrong with you? Jesus! Fool! Coward! Liar!

writes, pauses, sits down at the end of dining table without laptop and writes more

C'mon, goddammit, look! You just have to look! You're in it now. You chose this. This is everything you wanted. You asked for this. You chose this... Me, I did.

reflects a moment, continues more quietly

But no, I didn't. I never chose this, not *this*. There was never any choice. This just came out of nowhere, just crashed into me like a...

slams table

BAM!

she sweeps papers and debris off the table violently and buries her head in her arms, after a beat she emerges, stands, takes a calming breath, smiles, adjusts her hair and resumes pacing in small circuits

Okay, Julie, slow down, think a minute. This is it, this is exactly where you want to be. This is what it's all been for. Regardless of any other consideration, here you are, you are here. Here. Now. This is happening and there is no choice about anything. You're in total freefall. Can't stop, can't go back, can't even turn... like a bullet, like a train... on iron rails...

sits back down

But it can't be done. No one could do it, *I* certainly can't. No one could. Yeah, yeah, *he* did, but who knows about him? He doesn't even seem real at times... just someone I dreamed up...

yells upward

Aren't you?

stands, speaks forcefully to self

It *can* be done. It *has* been done. You will do it. You *must!* You can't *not...* it's as easy as falling... as easy as dying...

paces

No, no, no... stop lying to yourself... I was a fool to ever think it could be done... that I could do it... There is just no way... I can't do it, I can't take another step. I will physically tear my guts out before I continue this savage... emotional... mutilation... No! Stop it! Sit! Write! Think!

she sits, fusses with hair

Small steps, he said. One step at a time, he said. Yes, that's the only way... That's how I got this far and that's how I'll get further. Further, yes, further is everything, the only thing. One step, one little step, never look ahead, just worry about that next step... Stop yapping and focus goddammit!

*picks up her pad and pen, sits, writes,
thoughtful, more calm*

Yes, yes, there it is, that's it, that makes sense, keep going, you can do it... Is that it? Does that make sense?

*she stands, paces with the pad reading
what she just wrote, holding the pad
in one hand and conducting her
thoughts with the pen in the other
hand, quietly speaking what she reads,
very immersed...*

No, no, no, that's wrong... that's just, I'm just... is that right? It must be... but it can't be, can it? It must be... but how? If this is right then... If this is right, which it is, then... oh c'mon, please no, no. Stop. Stop. All you have to do is look, just look!

*stops, bends forward, takes deep
breaths*

Breathe, he tells me... like I'd forget to breathe... He said I didn't even know how to breathe...

straightens, puts attention on her
breathing, calms

Ha! I laugh! How can anyone not know how to breathe? Jesus, we don't stand a chance. One person who can help me and what does he say? Breathe, he says, take naps, drink water, don't resist…

yells upward

Big help!

a-ha moment

That's right… don't resist… he said that… don't resist. Am I resisting? I don't think so, I'm trying not to… Yes I'm resisting. Of *course* I'm resisting. I'm peeling off my own skin piece by piece, it's excruciating, how can I not resist? Small steps, that's how. One step at a time… don't look ahead… don't worry about success, just worry about the next small step… that's gonna take everything you've got.

goes to table, searches papers next to
laptop

Where is it, where is it…? Here it is. Here.

reading

"The pain comes from resisting. You can't *not* resist, but you can resist *less*, but don't resist the urge to resist."

she pauses to ponder that, continues

reading

"Surrender and allow, that's the key. Surrender, allow the process to unfold. When it's bad, you're fighting it. Stop fighting and let it happen. It's not a doing, it's an allowing." Okay, yes, I see that, but that doesn't mean I can do it...

looks back at pages, reads

"Yes, *you* can do it... it's the same for everyone... small steps, one small step at a time..." yeah, yeah, "sometimes when it comes off it comes off in layers."

tosses pages aside, happier now

Oh my God, that's right, it comes off in layers. That's what that means. Just grab a piece and peel and then all sorts of stuff... whoosh! Just gone.

in delight

Ha! I laugh! Stuff I thought would never be gone... just gone. And you don't even notice it's gone until you look. You look and say oh my God, I was so fucking intense about my... whatever... my career, my looks, my boyfriend, money, future, and now I can't even remember why. Did I ever really give a shit about that?

continues in wonder

And it's not painful or wrenching, you just look back and see all the shit that's just gone. These things that hung from me like lead weights, like baggage, like garbage. Where are they now? Who cares! Gone is all! How strange. I thought I'd have to scratch and claw through every little piece of crap, but sometimes they just... wash away... Gone, just gone.

> *clutches head*

Christ, my mind won't stop racing, I have to relax...

> *picks up a throw blanket and looks around. She drops the blanket and pushes the couch away from fireplace upstage opening the space and leaving the couch facing downstage. She spreads throw blanket on the floor in front of fire, tries to center herself, breathes, performs a yoga posture, attempts composure and breath control for several beats, then falls to the floor retching and pleading*

Oh my God! Oh my God! What have I done? Mother! Mommy! Mommy! Oh no no no... Mommy, pleee-ase... I want to go home...

> *curls up in a fetal ball on the floor, sobbing and rocking, cradling the throw blanket like a doll, guttural bursts, finally rises to sitting, hunched, weary, spent*

Months of this, months and months... and for what? So far to go, no way out, just falling, endless falling...

How far? This can't go on... *I* can't go on.

sniffs, laughs derisively

Stupid! Don't look ahead... Ha!

rolls up onto knees, powering up again

He did it. He did. But he's a freak, an anomaly... He had some advantage, something different, but that's him, not me... What's my advantage? I have no advantage... I'm going to die, no other way. Maybe that's my advantage, the certainty of failure, the inevitability of failure. Yes, there's a freedom in that... in certainty. That's fine. Just as well. Can't run home to mommy... no going back... Burn your bridges, he said; consciously, deliberately, with malice aforethought. That's what he said. Burn it all.

stands, holding blanket, head down,
thinking, processing

Go back? Ha! Wouldn't if I could. Back? Back to what? Back to some primitive state I called life? Never gonna happen, no way. Humans can't go back to being monkeys and I can't go back to being human.

tosses blanket onto couch, paces,
speaks thoughtfully, sanely

I'd rather die than go back. Yes, there, that was easy enough... and it's true, that's what matters. It's the truth. I'd rather die doing this than live like I was. I'd rather fail at this than succeed at anything else. That's true, that's my power, that's my advantage. It must have been his too. What other advantage could there be? Destiny? Fate? Karma? Bullshit! What else is there? Failure is my advantage. Death is my advantage.

realization

Oh shit, that's surrender! That's what he said. Surrender. Free from hope, free from desire, free from expectation. I can't die if I'm already dead.

she wraps herself in the throw blanket,
curls up on couch

Rest, I have to remember to rest. When did I sleep? Who knows. Day, night, day, night... is there still a world out there? Was there ever? How could I be so wrong? What a fool, but no more. I do this or I die trying, clean and simple. My life is completely blown to pieces, completely shattered, but for the first time it all makes sense.

fading

Do or die. I don't care which, but no more of what it was. That's over forever.

nearly asleep

All I want is to cut myself out of these tangled nets of...

sits up, alert

Food! Eat! I have to remember to eat. Powerbars and

good water, he said...

> *she picks up an open powerbar*
> *from the floor, unwraps, takes a bite,*
> *rewraps, tosses it back*

There, I ate. Happy? Oh, that's right, I crashed for a few hours a few days ago. That was nice. Took a shower, ate some soup, almost felt clean... then it started again. Was that only a few days ago? Maybe a week. Seems like a lifetime... seems like I was different person then... Don't look back. Why look back? Trust the process, he says. There's higher things at work, he says. Observe the pattern, he says. Yes, I understand, but it doesn't help when this sickness comes, when my guts get all twisted up and my brain starts burning and the energy is too much for my body....

> *stands, goes to laptop, speaks as she*
> *types*

Email ninety-, what?, ninety-two? Hey, are you there? I know you're not but I think you are. I spoke to Cathy yesterday, she called to make sure her little sister's okay. She asked me if I thought I was cracking up and I was so tired I accidentally told the truth. I said "What the fuck do I care?" I guess I've been saying that a lot lately because she got all pissy and asked if that was my answer to everything. She was just asking rhetorically, but I thought about it for a moment and realized that yes, actually, that *is* my answer to everything. It was one of those awesome moments of clarity that light up a dark corner you thought could never be clean. What the fuck do I care? Ahhh. It's like taking a long overdue bath and washing away layers of grime that were hardened like a crust and you come out all pink and fresh and ten pounds lighter. *In* the world but not *of* the world, you said. That's what I am now. I'm not mean or evil or bad, I'm simply no longer *of* the world, I am a thing apart. What a liberating realization! How nice to shed all that filth and be so clean. Thanks sis! I guess you never know where it's gonna come from. Send!

> *she stands and starts picking up pieces*
> *of paper off the table and the floor,*
> *examining some briefly, keeping one or*
> *two, strolls to fireplace, reads from a*
> *page slowly and thoughtfully*

"If thy right eye offendeth thee, pluck it out, if thy right hand offendeth thee, cut it off and cast it from thee, for 'tis better to have one eye..." yeah, yeah... "for 'tis better that the members should perish than the whole body be cast into hellfire..."

> *balls sheet and throws in fire*

That's this alright. Cut off the offensive part to save the... save the what? What's left to save when all the parts offend? Nothing. Nothing is saved, nothing is fixed, nothing is made better. So what's the point? There is no point, I knew that in the first moment when this whole thing started... I am already dead.

I keep thinking I'm supposed to be becoming something but I'm really becoming nothing.... seems like a lot to go through just to become nothing.

> *returns to laptop, sits and begins*
> *writing while speaking*

Email ninety-uh... three. Am I insane? I wonder. I know I'm not, but that doesn't mean I'm not. It's okay if I am, I wouldn't mind... it's actually kind of comforting, I could wrap myself in insanity like a warm blanket. I'm certainly talking to myself a lot, but it doesn't seem crazy. It seems natural and necessary, like if I didn't talk I would explode... Maybe that's how crazy people see it... like maybe they see things in a way no one else does so they have to tell someone, but they only have themselves to talk to. Only they understand themselves... Is that me? I definitely see things... *way* different from everyone else, except for you and I might have imagined you... so yeah, that sounds pretty crazy. If anyone were watching me now they'd definitely think I was – what would it be? schizo? manic? bi-polar? – I mean, screaming and crying one minute, writing the next, puking the next, calm and normal the next, and then it starts again... and again and again, day after day, for months now! And no end in sight. That's *gotta* be crazy... and here's the kicker, here's the one that seals the deal, the final nail in the crazy coffin; I absolutely, positively believe that I am sane and everyone else is insane. There's no getting away from that one. I can't even deny it. It'd be pretty funny if it weren't so goddamn funny. Send!

she stands and stares at her laptop
for a beat, then picks up a messy pile
of papers and walks slowly to the
fireplace

What if I *am* crazy?

speaking in short bursts while scanning
pages

Crazy is okay. Not so bad. Some parts bad. Some parts good. Crazy life. Crazy me. Live on the street. People do. Have my own shopping cart. It can be done. Become an addict, a hooker, both, whatever. Doesn't matter. Only *this* matters. There is nothing else. There is only this. Whatever. I can go on. Whatever.

throws a few pages into fire

I say I can go on, but that's just bullshit cheerleader talk.

peppy

Rah rah, you go girl!

normal again

Trying to get my game face on, convince myself it can be done when I'm not looking, but as soon as I *do* look I know it can't be done. Still, I have to keep going… no stopping, no turning back, no hope of getting out alive… no hope. What a life… I was a girl, a person, a daughter, a sister, a citizen. I had a life, friends, a career… all gone… plans, marriage, love, motherhood... all gone. Do I miss them?

pause to consider

No. There is no me left to miss anything. That part is gone.

> *she walks back to her desk, on top of*
> *the printer is a stack of papers like a*
> *manuscript, an inch think, she thumbs*
> *through it, pausing here and there,*
> *shaking her head in disgust*

My manifesto. Can't be crazy without a good rambling manifesto explaining why the whole world is crazy and I'm the only sane one.

> *strolls back to fireplace while reading,*
> *tosses a few pages at a time into the*
> *fire*

This was, what, the seventh draft? Tenth? I lost track... Who cares? Who's it for? Me? Him? I'm the only one left. There's only me and I'm long gone.

> *tosses more pages in fireplace*

Maybe the next version.

> *tosses the rest of manuscript in fire,*
> *yells to unseen someone above*

Can you hear me?! I called the suicide hotline last night just to talk... Got a message. Ha! I laugh. Budget cuts. You said you wouldn't let me cling to you... that it wasn't your job to save me but to let me drown...

quietly

No one can save me... nothing to save...

wraps shoulders in throw blanket and
paces, softer now, almost romantic

Maybe tonight I'll sit out again, sit in the rocker on the porch, wrapped in a blanket, looking up at the stars and thinking about death. Not just death... *my* death. My one true friend. None of this would be possible without the thought of death. If I didn't know death was always so near, so close...

puts her right hand on her left shoul-
der, as if on death's everpresent hand,
sits in the rocker in front of the fire,
rocks gently for a few moments

They don't tell you about this. They don't tell you because they don't know. But why don't they know? It's all so obvious. What could be more obvious than this? This is literally the most obvious possible thing. How is this, of all things, a mystery? Why don't they teach this in school?

stands, still wrapped in blanket, speaks
in a frantic rant, like all one sentence,
while pacing in short circuits

History, math, science, are you kidding? Oh my god! Who could possibly care about any of that crap?

How can they be so... so vapid? So unconscious? Is it some sort of joke? Some conspiracy? A conspiracy to do what? What is accomplished? What is the end result? Cui bono? Cui bono? All of humanity stays in a state of... rancid dismay, fatuous ignorance, bloated torpor...

stops short

Torpor? Were did that word come from? I don't think I ever used that word before...

grabs a dictionary off the mantle, finds the word and reads

"Torpor: sluggish, lethargic, dormant, like a hibernating animal." Well, that's the right word alright. Where did it come from? I never used it before.

replaces dictionary, resumes pacing, slow, thoughtful

There's more at work here, he said. Something more than me, some overlighting something. I see it now. I used to see it a little here and there, now and then, but now I seem to see it everywhere, all the time. It's not a doing, it's an allowing, he says, and that's right because whenever I allow, it just unfolds perfectly... every time... better than I could ever do. Yes, there's more at work here... *Bullshit!* I'm just stalling now, looking up words, trying to take a step back and observe... trying to act sane, shut out the storm...

mania building again

This, right now, this is the calm. Ha! I laugh. This is the calm but the storm rages on. It comes. It comes. I feel it, it's already churning my guts. I don't know how I survived the last and now... now another... Too much, way too much, can't be done... Why can't this just be over? It will never be over...

rushes to laptop

Write to him again... he told me to... as much as I need... part of the process...

drops blanket, shakes out hands to dispel excess energy, sits at laptop and speaks as she types

Are you there? Do you exist? This is my, let's see, ninety-*fourth* email to you. Do you read them? Do you even know I sent them? Are you really out there? Are you just a part of the dreamworld I woke up from, or are you the one real thing? I have to think you're real even though we both know you're not... Maybe you're my death. Ha! That's a heartwarming thought. You're with me now, hand on my shoulder. That's a comfort, but it's just sentimental bullshit! I can't indulge in any kind of bullshit anymore. The slightest whiff sends me on a total freakout. I'm between storms for the moment. I thought I got myself to solid ground but already I can feel it slipping away. I'm trying to hold it back but it's coming. I try not to look.

rereads what she has typed, mouthing the words, speaking quietly and quickly

Vomit. Emotional puke. Gorging and disgorging. Spiritual bulimia. Fuck it. Don't read it, don't fix it, just send it. Send!

stands, looks around tiredly, sits to write again, speaks as she types

Shit. Ninety-five. I swing slowly back and forth between crushing fatigue and shrieking mania. This aching tiredness though... my body can't keep up. I've probably lost thirty pounds, I'm down three sizes, maybe four. My face is gaunt, my clothes don't fit. I know I should eat, go for walks, get some rest... but it just seems so irrelevant. Ha! I laugh. Relevant to what? There's nothing left to be relevant to. I am damned. Damned for looking, for doubting, damned for asking why. Send.

she stands and walks to a wall mirror, speaks to her reflection in old lady voice, wags finger scoldingly

"You always seemed like such a sensible girl. Look at you now. How exactly does one manage to fall off the planet, dear?"

turns away from mirror

I look like hell... so what... it doesn't matter how I look and it will never matter again. My time among the humans is over....

lifts a bottle of whiskey from a shelf

Maybe this would make it easier.

sets it back down

I don't want it to be easier, I want it to be harder. Not in dribs and drabs...

big, chest-thumping arm gestures

I want it all! Now! Full force! Kill me with it! This is it! This is everything, the *only* thing, here, now, waiting for me to find it... I know I won't find it... I know there's nothing to find... I knew that from the very first second back... back...

looks upward

...back when I was still with you.

pauses, reflects, sits and speaks as she types

Ninety-six. You told me what to do. You said that the only way to win was not to fight. The only power it has is the power I give it, you said so... so, fine! I strip off my armor. I drop my sword and walk naked into the flames.

rereads last sentence in a low voice

Ewww, yuck! Sorry for the poetic bullshit, but I promised I wouldn't edit myself so I'll leave it in... Don't identify with your character, you said, separate the actor from the character, but what is an actor without a role to play? Nothing, a cipher, zero, the absence of presence.

pauses, reflects, types

You were right, it's not about courage, is it? Or cowardice either... Just fear and slow death. Just a slow sinking into a warm bath of acid... That which is exposed shall burn away, and all will be exposed. Nothing hidden, nothing withheld... No choice...

ponders, types

Was there ever a choice? I don't remember a time when I chose. I didn't choose this. No one would ever choose this. But here I am. Careful what you wish for. Send.

stands, agitated, drinks from a water bottle, sits back down and types as she speaks

Ninety-seven. My friend, my only friend, the time approaches when I must feed you to the flames as well. I know it. I have known the end since the beginning. Here in a place of childhood laughter I continue my mad descent into sanity. That's okay. It's over, just as it should be. It is the end of things. Such days must come and these are those days. It must be and it is. I am both consumer and consumed, but what remains when the terrible meal is over?

quietly, upward

And who will we be, we who know war, who will we

be when war is gone?

beat

Who cares? None of my business. I have a job to do and everything else is a stall tactic. I dissolve in my own acids. I digest myself. Send.

*stands, paces, sits again, types as she
speaks*

Shit. Ninety-eight. One more thing while I have you... My mistake is thinking that I might somehow survive, or that I even want to. There's no surviving this. This is it, this is the end. I am falling to my death and there's nothing I can do but fall. The outcome was certain since the falling began, since I was with you. Send.

stands, walks to couch, flops

Brace for impact, he said. Smart ass. An impact is over in a split second, that's nothing compared to this end-less falling. No more, no more. I'm done. That's what this is, the end... the end of something that never was. It's ridiculously true, I am a zombie, a living but uninhabited body.

eyes closed, speaking as if in prayer

This too shall pass... This too shall pass... This too shall pass...

*jarring phone ring, older grating bell,
she jumps*

Jesus!

> *another ring, she clears her throat and
> tests her bright cheerful voice*

One, two, one, two, three.

> *ring, she makes a phone of her hand*

Hi!

> *croaky, coughs*

Hi mom!

> *cough*

Hi mom, yes, fine! Yeah everything's...

> *ring*

...great!

> *stops trying*

Shit, I sound like I look.

> *adjusts her hair, phone rings again and
> stops mid-ring, she stands, paces*

Gotta talk to her... gotta convince her I'm okay. Can't
have anyone showing up to check on me... stick me
in a hospital... seven day psych-eval... Ha! That might
be nice... a medication vacation...

> *holds imaginary phone to ear, tries
> voice*

Hi mom! Yeah, it's going great!

clears throat

Hi! Mom! Yeah, yeah, it's going great!

clears throat, drinks water

Hi mom! Yeah, everything's fine here, just what I need!

massages throat, trying to get her happy voice back

The book? Oh, great! It's really coming along... really catching my stride. Oh, a few more months at least...

facade cracking

Great, great, everything's great! Just great! Just fuckin' great, mom! No mom, there's no book, that's just what I told you to get the cabin. No mom, no more career, no more dreams of being a writer... No mom, I don't think I'll be finding a man and settling down anytime soon. No mom, sorry, I think babies are off the table too, sorry... so sorry... sorry to disappoint. Yeah mom, funny thing happened... I'm going through a little something, ha!... no, no, just a little meltdown... no, sorry, not the kind you come back from... no, sorry mom, one way trip, sorry to disappoint... your daughter got caught up in some weird zombie vampire undead shit and now she's gone gone gone... You caught me at a bad time... I was just in the middle of killing you, mommy, slicing you out of my heart like a tumor... Yes, mother! I know what it sounds like. I know exactly what it sounds like! It sounds totally batshit fuckin' crazy cuz that's exactly what I am!

softer

Goodbye mommy.

hangs up imaginary phone

I need more practice.

> *she stands, enters kitchen, comes*
> *out with a bottled water like others*
> *littering the room, opens, drinks, set it*
> *down absently*

A shower would make me feel better, a shower, a nap, a walk in the woods. That's what he'd say; go for walks, breathe correctly, get some rest. Yeah, that would make me feel better, all clean and fresh, but I don't want to be clean and fresh. I want to be muddy and bloody and raw. I want to remember where I am. I don't want to slip off on a little R&R. This doesn't wait. I don't want to go drink a latte or see a movie, I don't want to know what's going on in the world, I don't want to know how anyone is doing... Ha! How can anyone watch a movie or a play or laugh or go to work or do anything with this massive black ball of cancerous shit coating their soul? I don't want to think about anyone or be thought of by anyone or spend a single minute doing anything other than this.

pauses, looks around suspiciously

It's quiet now but that's just a trick. The calm before the storm. The pattern, always the pattern, flowing and bending, folding and reforming. As soon as you think you're okay and try to relax you get that first little tingle, that first little warning that it's starting again, that first little twitch...

phone rings, she jerks, startled

Yeah, like that.

ring

Jesus, what do they want? These people. Don't they know? Can't they sense it?

ring

Can't they tell I'm gone? Can't they feel the empty space where I used to be?

ring

They're like demons to me now, clingy little tormentors...

ring

...voices from the past, clawing at me...

half ring

...trying to pull me back down. I hear them calling, incessantly calling – RING! RING! RING! – and I have such an urge to answer, to respond, to climb back down into the darkness and grapple with them, but I can't. I must get to light, not crawl back down into that putrid sewer...

> *she's up and getting frantic, bouncing*
> *off the walls, shaking out her arms,*
> *building up energy with no outlet*

I'd like to go for a walk but we're not supposed to go out at night without the dog, but she just wants to stay on her bed these days.

voice of child mocking parents

Stay close at night, children. Bears are out at night and they like to eat little girls!

normal again

Do they? Do bears eat little girls? That wouldn't be bad. Eaten by a bear... eaten by a bear... hmmm. I wonder if they kill you or just rip your face off? Face ripped off is not a good look for me. Maybe struck by lightning... how bad could that be? Over like that...

snaps

...and it sounds pretty cool. Nothin' left but smoking shoes. Eaten by bear... struck by lightning... bear, lightning, hmm, both sound okay. What else is there? Rabid squirrel. Yuck. Nasty corpse, but what corpse isn't nasty? Swept down river in a flash flood, body not recovered. Ha! Not recovered sounds better than mauled or fried! Fell from a ladder while picking fruit? Too poetic, too pastoral. What about self-digested? Leaving no trace... yes, that's the one. She simply consumed herself... Death by honesty. *Poof!* Gone as if she never was...

> *stops energetic movement, tries to*
> *calm, shake off energy, can't, doubles*
> *over, smashes fist against leg*

Fuck you, you whining fool. You coward, you pathetic weakling. The nastier the corpse the better. Rotten stinking bloated maggot-infested...

> *bends, hands on knees*

...fuck all pretty thoughts...

> *on the edge of hyperventilating*

...fuck this bullshit inside me... fuck how it got there... fuck that part of me that protects it... fuck this whole goddamn stinking mess.

> *stands slowly, rigidly*

How do you like your little princess now, daddy? How do you like your little ballerina now, mommy? Try not to entertain negativity, they say. Ha! I can't entertain enough negativity. I have become a fire-breathing dragon of negativity. There is nothing I won't burn, nothing I won't destroy. With malice aforethought, goddamn right. There's no stopping this. There's no hiding from this, not *this*, *never* this...

resumes deep breaths, becomes calm,
speaks deliberately

I said to myself, Look! I have experienced much of wisdom and knowledge, and also of madness and folly, and I learned that this, too, is a chasing after wind.

agitated pacing

Breathe, relax, it's coming, I feel it and I know what it is. It's exactly what I didn't want it to be. The exact thing I didn't want it to be is exactly what it is. I tried not to look... Too soon... too much... It can't happen... it can't be stopped... So this is how it finally ends...

goes to window, looks out

Imagine being afraid of death... Ha! Was I?, I was, but that wasn't me, that was her. I'm not afraid of the dark, I'm afraid of the light; the terrible cold light where everything is completely visible and there's nowhere left to hide...

turns away from window

Yes, here it comes...

walks to mirror, speaks weakly

All I ever did... all I did was ask why.

inspects reflection, speaks strongly

Don't be fooled by appearances! You're not some little girl playing out her little girl dreams anymore...

turns away from mirror, transforms

I am a soldier now, a *true* warrior! I have a single objective... I am locked on like a laser. Survival is irrelevant. I will locate this cancer in me and I will destroy it... all such cancers, wherever they grow, whatever they look like... family, future, dreams beliefs, fears, my very heart... Yes, if my heart offendeth me I shall pluck it out and cast it from me. Burn it all. What I've dared, I've willed and what I've willed, I'll do! How can the prisoner reach outside except by thrusting through the wall?

*hits wall switches to dim the room,
strides to front and center, powerfully*

Captain on the bridge! All hands to battle stations! Red alert!

adopts a command posture

This is not a drill, people. This is some real-world, ask-no-questions, take-no-prisoners shit. We're going in!

*laughs crazily and shakes arms and
hands as if to release energy*

Ha! Goddamn right we're going in. This is it, people, no more tomorrows! It has been a pleasure serving with you. Brace for impact! Here we go. Rock 'n roll!

stands down, paces, hands on hips,

speaks with energy

That's right, that's exactly right. I am the captain of this ship and this is the one true war and we are fresh out of tomorrows. Every drop, every ounce, nothing in reserve, nothing held back... Ramming speed!

pauses, turns forward and throws arms back, chest forward, as if exposing breastbone to unseen sword

Here I am. I lower my shield, expose my heart. I am open. I will not relent. I will not go back a single inch. Slay me!

releases posture, pulls her hair back tight and ties it

Ha! This is it, this is the war, this is the game. There is only this, there was *always... only... this.* Now I know. There is nothing I won't do, nothing I won't burn, no one I won't put to the torch.

upward

Even you. When the time comes, even you.

back to pacing

The path to my fixed purpose is laid with iron rails whereon my soul is grooved to run. Goddamn right it is.

speaking deliberately, through clenched teeth

The path to my fixed purpose... is laid with iron rails... whereon my soul... is grooved... to run.

*laughs a bit maniacally, pulls off
sweater, still pacing, now in gray sports
bra and jeans, hair tight back*

The path to my fixed purpose is laid with iron rails. Yes it is. And on those iron rails my soul is grooved to run. Despite everything, regardless of the pain, the loss, the certainty of the outcome, I am the happiest I have ever been, the happiest it is possible to be.

*strips off jeans and throws them aside,
now in matching gray underwear,
faces front, faces destiny, raises hands
slowly, like a kid with shaky balance
letting go of handlebars for the first
time*

This is what it means to be in control. I control nothing yet I am in perfect control. I know nothing, yet nothing is unknown. My surrender is absolute and my victory assured. C'mon you bastards, you loves and lovers, you lovely dreams and dreams of love, all to doom! All to flames and ash! There is only this and even as it shreds my heart and rips my soul to pieces there is no place I'd rather be. Ha! I laugh!

throws arms up in victory

I have already won!

lights fade

Intermission 5

Guy

Yeah, me. Jesus, wow, that one was fucked up. I have
no idea what I just saw. Listen, by the way, I uh, I don't
have a massive ball of black shit coating my soul like
a cancer, do I? I mean, no, never mind, stupid question, I know… Theater, right? Yeah, no shit… You ever
wonder if it's all theater and we're all just… what? No,
yeah, we're still on for the game…

*Guy and Girl wander close to each
other*

Hold on, I can't hear you, whatshername can't stop
yappin' into her phone every time there's a break…
can't just be alone with her thoughts for a minute…
I know, right?

Girl

annoyed by Guy, terse wave, turns and
moves away

Jeez, this guy's really grinding my nuts. The play? I don't know, the first one was cute, with these babies and everything, then the next one was like war and torture and some like philosophy stuff or whatever, then there was like a funny parade thing and then a weird debate thing, but this last one was totally... I don't know, it's getting a little too... something... I'm not sure I like theater. I hope the next one is...

music starts

Shit, gotta go...

ACT VI: FEDALLAH

Transition music, sung by kids:

> oh! jolly is the gale,
> and a joker is the whale,
> just a' flourishin' his tail,
> such a funny, sporty, gamy, jesty,
>   hoky-poky joker is the whale, oh!

> when the black storm clouds arise,
> and the lightning cracks the skies,
> then he nearly splits his sides,
> such a funny, sporty, gamy, jesty,
>   hoky-poky joker is the whale, oh!

> when the thunder rolls and rips,
> to the splinterin' of ships,
> and he only smacks his lips,
> such a funny, sporty, gamy, jesty,
>   hoky-poky joker is the whale, oh!

SETTING

Quarterdeck of the Pequod. Day. A soft but distinct sun setting behind red and black clouds.

CHARACTERS

AHAB: Captain. Spent, grizzled, burnt, gray, charred, ashen. Missing leg replaced with whalebone.

STARBUCK: First Mate. Young, handsome, courageous, decent.

FEDALLAH: A shadowy figure staring malevolently out from a dark corner, holding harpoon. Large face and head, high braided black hair, darkly exotic, demonic red eyes. Only visible as called for.

> *Ahab paces back and forth on the*
> *quarterdeck, step-THUMP, step-*
> *THUMP, boot and whalebone leg,*
> *stops to lean on rail and contemplate*
> *the sea, facing audience.*

Ahab

Where lies the final harbor, whence we unmoor no more? In what rapt ether sails the world of which the weariest will never weary?

Forty, forty, forty years ago! Forty years of continual whaling! Forty years of privation and peril and storm-time! Forty years on the pitiless sea! For forty years has Ahab forsaken the peaceful land to make war on the horrors of the deep!

What is it? What nameless, inscrutable, unearthly thing is it? What hidden lord and master commands me that against all natural lovings and longings I keep pushing myself on, recklessly making me do what in my own proper heart I would not so much as dare?

slams hand down on rail

Great God! We are turned round and round in this world like yonder windlass, and Fate is the handspike. Is Ahab Ahab? Is it I, God, that lifts this arm? But if the great sun move not of himself, and is but an errand-boy in heaven, then how can this one small heart beat, this one small brain think, unless God does that beating, God does that thinking? And if not God, then who?

*turns to face FEDALLAH, red eyes in a
dark face staring silently back at him*

Forty years! Aye! And then the madness, the frenzy, the boiling blood and the smoking brow with which for a thousand hunts has old Ahab chased his prey, more a demon than a man! Aye, aye! What a forty years' fool has old Ahab been! Why this strife of the chase? Why weary the arm at the oar and the lance? How richer or better is Ahab now? But silence! Comes the First Mate.

Starbuck

*Starbuck on stairs to quarterdeck and
Ahab, soliloquy*

I come to report a fair wind, but how fair? Fair for the
hunt of Moby Dick, fair for death and doom. Aye, for
this hunt would Ahab gladly kill all his crew, but shall
I suffer this crazed old man to drag a whole ship's
company down to doom? It would make him the
murderer of thirty men if this ship comes to deadly
harm, and come to deadly harm my soul swears it will
if Ahab has his way. He'll swamp us all, boat and crew,
in his mad pursuit of the white whale.

*withdraws a small pistol, clearly
coming to kill Ahab, falters, continues
soliloquy*

Heart of wrought steel, canst thou yet ring boldly?
Great God! Is this my journey's end? The past grows
dim. Mary, Mary! Thou fadest in pale glory. Boy, son! I
see thine eyes, now grown wondrous blue.

strengthens

Feel thy heart, Starbuck. Stir thyself! Move! Where's
the old man now? See'st thou Ahab? Hear'st his ivory
foot upon the deck?

*Starbuck steps onto quarterdeck and
approaches Ahab's back, pistol rigidly
outstretched until it is an inch from
Ahab's head*

God is against thee, old man. Forbear! It is not too late, even now, to desist. 'Tis an ill voyage, ill begun and ill continued. Let me square the yards while we may, and make a fair wind of it homewards, to go on a better voyage than this.

Ahab

as if he hadn't heard

Oh Starbuck! Is it not hard that with this weary load I bear, one poor leg should have been snatched from under me? Here, brush this old hair aside. It blinds me that I seem to weep. Locks so grey did never grow but from out of ashes!

> *Starbuck softens, lowers the gun and tucks it in his waist, Ahab turns to face him*

But do I look so very, very old, Starbuck? I feel deadly faint, bowed and humped, as though I were Adam staggering beneath the piled centuries since Paradise. God! Crack my heart! Stave my brain!

> *Ahab clasps Starbuck's shoulders and pulls him close*

Close! Stand close to me, Starbuck, let me look into a human eye. 'Tis better than to gaze upon God. This is the magic glass, man. I see my wife in thine eye. I see my child, my boy. His mother tells him of me, how I am abroad upon the deep, but will yet come back to dance him once again.

Starbuck

*joyously relieved, clasps Ahab's
shoulder*

Oh Captain, my Captain! Noble soul! Grand old heart
after all! Why should we continue to give chase to
that hated fish? Away with us! Let us fly these deadly
waters! Away! Let us away! This instant let me alter the
course! How cheerily, how hilariously, O my Captain,
will we set sail to see old Nantucket again!

Ahab

*darkens, hardens, pushes Starbuck's
hand away*

No, Mr. Starbuck, no.

*pushes Starbuck away, Starbuck tries
to reconnect*

I tell thee no, it cannot be. If thou speakest thus to me
much more, Ahab's purpose keels up in him! There is
that in thee, Starbuck, which I feel too curing to my
malady, and for this hunt, my malady becomes my
most desired health. Death to Moby Dick! God hunt
us all if we do not hunt Moby Dick to his death!

Starbuck

steps back, stricken

Moby Dick seeks thee not old man! It is thou that
madly seekest him! You will kill us all with your mad

vengeance upon a dumb brute that smote thee from blindest instinct! Madness!

Ahab

step/thumps to Fedallah, snatches harpoon, returns and thrusts it menacingly at Starbuck

Hark ye, Nantucketer! Here in this hand I hold the white whale's death! Tempered by lightning! Baptized in the melted bones of murderers!

turns away, soliloquy

He thinks me mad, Starbuck does, but I am madness maddened! That wild madness that's only calm to comprehend itself! These men think old Ahab would kill a fish for vengeance' sake, but they are as cogs in the great wheel turning irresistibly to doom. To doom at last, all to doom! Aye, but who's to doom when the judge himself is dragged to the bar?

turns back to Starbuck

Hark ye yet again, Starbuck, the little lower layer. All visible objects are but as pasteboard masks. If man will strike, strike through the mask! How can the prisoner reach outside except by thrusting through the wall? To me, the white whale is that wall!

aside

Sometimes I think there's naught beyond... but 'tis enough.

Starbuck

Great God! Shall we keep chasing this murderous fish till he swamps the last man? Shall we be dragged by him to the bottom of the sea? Shall we be towed by him to the infernal world? Oh, impiety and blasphemy to hunt him more!

Ahab

Talk not to me of blasphemy, man; I'd strike the sun if it insulted me! Who's over me? Truth hath no confines!

softens

Thou art but too good a fellow, Starbuck, but Ahab is forever Ahab. This whole act is immutably decreed. 'Twas rehearsed by thee and me a billion years before this ocean rolled.

Starbuck

Captain, I beg of thee...

Ahab

Fool! I am the Fates' lieutenant. I act under orders!

points to pistol in Starbuck's waist

Say ye that I should beware of Starbuck?

Starbuck

backing away

Ahab need not beware of Starbuck, but let Ahab beware of Ahab. Beware of thyself, old man.

Starbuck exits

Ahab

the sky darkens, thunder begins to roll,
lightning flashes. Ahab points harpoon
upward as if addressing God

I now know thee, thou clear spirit, and I know that thy right worship is defiance. To neither love nor reverence wilt thou be kind. Even for hate thou can but kill, and all are kill'd. Thy lightning flashes through my skull, my brain is scorched, my eyeballs ache. Thou art light leaping out of darkness, but I am darkness leaping out of light! Of thy fire thou madest me, and like a true child of fire, I breathe it back to thee!

to Fedallah

What I've dared, I've willed, and what I've willed, I'll do! The path to my fixed purpose is laid with iron rails whereon my soul is grooved to run. Over unsounded gorges, through the rifled hearts of mountains, under torrents' beds, unerringly I rush! Naught's an obstacle, naught's an angle to the iron way!

returns to rail, looking out over sea and
audience

For forty years has Ahab forsaken the peaceful land, for forty years to make war on the horrors of the deep! Have a care, all ye fools and madmen, for Ahab too is mad! Listen, and thou wilt often hear my ivory foot upon the deck, and still know that I am there.

slams harpoon on deck

And now I quit thee!

lights fade

INTERMISSION 6

Guy

Yeah, whassup? Yeah, still going... this last thing was like a weird *Moby-Dick* remix... no, not Moby, Moby Dick. What? No, Moby Dick. Dick Dick DICK!

sees Girl watching him suspiciously,
points at phone sheepishly

Yeah, the whale thing, ever read it? Well, I read it but this was different, but not really, know what I mean? I mean, like, I don't know, maybe I didn't really get it...

Girl

Geez, I just wanted a nice night out, you know? A few drinks, maybe some... yeah, right, but now it's like, c'mon already? This last one was like Captain Ahab for chrissakes! No, not Star Trek, the book, you know, like with the guy trying to kill the whale? No, no, where do you get Free Willy from what I said? The whale book, Moby Dick, no, not him, Dick! DICK!

Guy looks over, she points to her
phone sheepishly

Guy

I think she's into me.

Girl

Great, now he thinks I'm into him.

Guy

Hell no, I'm not really gonna read *Moby Dick* again. I barely survived it the first time and that was skipping over most of it. This did seem familiar, though, like it was all really from the book, just messed with, like in a different order or something... No, no, I'm not, like, into it or anything, it's just, you know, maybe it's interesting or maybe there's more to it or something...

Girl

No, I don't think there's more to it. I mean, like what, some big meaning? It's just a bunch of pieces that don't fit together... The author? I don't know, some New Age guy or something, wrote some books, never heard of him, probably got bored writing books about meditation or horoscopes or whatever so now he writes this stupid play that doesn't make any sense...

Guy

What? No way, are you kidding? Nobody gets laid after a night like this, they probably just go home and wonder if the play sucked or they were just too dumb to get it. Shoulda just went dancing and got her drunk, coulda been asleep by now…

music starts

Both

Oh shit, there's more.

ACT VII: DELPHI

Transition music, sung by kids as a round:

> *row, row, row your boat,*
> *gently down the stream,*
> *merrily, merrily, merrily, merrily,*
> *life is but a dream*

CHARACTERS

MAN: Dressed in white hospital scrubs, barefoot. Up and in motion.

ORACLE: Draped in veils. Lounging regally on a high, throne-like chaise of tumbled stones.

SETTING

Ancient stone ruins. Desolate, colorless. The words KNOW THYSELF! are inscribed on a cracked and fallen arch.

A dozen or so tattered veils hang singly and in twos and threes, here and there. Soft air motion keeps them gently swaying.

Background: Audience left: There is a mansion on a hill, projected on a tattered veil. Audience right: There is a door marked EXIT, projected on an untattered veil.

Man

scrambling around examining his surroundings in a panic

Where am I? How did I get here? Am I dreaming? Is this a dream?

Oracle

So hard to know.

Man

Man freezes, searches for source of voice, speaks in all directions, not directly to Oracle

Where are you? Who are you?

Oracle

Who are you?

Man

I... I'm not sure.

Oracle

Man? Woman? Young? Old?

Man

I... I don't know.

Oracle

You don't know who you are?

Man

I have memories of being someone, someone I used to be, or it might have been a dream. How can I be sure?

Oracle

How can you be sure of anything?

Man

I don't know! Where are you?

Oracle

Oracle speaks in a singsong lilt as if repeating things she's said many times before, or as if speaking to a child

Here. With you. Always with you.

Man

What is this place?

Oracle

Whatever it seems to be.

Man

That's no answer. Who are you?

Oracle

I am the one you hear.

Man

Not big on straight answers, are you?

Oracle

Ask a straight question.

Man

The riddle thing gets old.

Oracle

All riddles are of your own making.

Man

Okay then, what was this place before I arrived?

Oracle

How could there be this without you?

Man

Riddles! Okay, arrived from where, then? Where am I from? How did I get here?

indicates mansion

Did I come from that house? Did I wander away from the party? Or am I asleep? Am I only dreaming this?

Oracle

Are you asking a question?

Man

Do you know the answer?

Oracle

Do you know the question?

Man

More riddles! How do I get out of here? Straight question.

Oracle

indifferently

If you think you're asleep, try waking up. If you think you wandered away, try wandering back.

Man

indicates veiled doorway marked EXIT

What about that door? Where does that lead?

Oracle

It's beyond me.

Man

Beyond you? What does that mean? What's on the other side of that door?

Oracle

That door has only one side.

Man approaches door, reaches out, hesitates, turns back

Man

Who else is here? Where is everyone?

Oracle

As you see.

Man

But the people! Where are the people?

Oracle

I have no knowledge.

> *Man explores the area, finds inscribed arch*

Man

And this! What's this?

Oracle

What does it seem to be?

Man

It seems to be from the Temple at Delphi.

Oracle

Then that.

Man

Are you the oracle?

Oracle

How would I know?

Man

It says Know Thyself.

Oracle

Ironic.

Man

But it's split, cracked, shattered.

Oracle

Ironicker still.

Man

What does it mean? Why did it crack?

Oracle

Perhaps it was unsound.

Man

Unsound as stone? Or unsound as an ontological imperative?

Oracle

Yes, perhaps.

Man

You're not very helpful.

Oracle

It's not my role to be helpful.

Man

Aha! What is your role, then?

Oracle

My role is what I do.

Man

Nothing but riddles.

moves toward mansion

What is that house? Is that where I came from? It seems like there's a party in progress, or is it a trick of light?

moves one way

From here it seems the house is settled for the night.

moves the other way

And from here it seems like... like a carnival! Answer me. What is it?

Oracle

It is what it seems to be. What else?

Man

I'm not asking what it seems to be, I'm asking what it is!

Oracle

There is no is, there is only seems.

Man

No, there is an actual house.

points

There it is! Right there! How can you say it's not?

Oracle

How can you say it is?

Man

I see it!

Oracle

You see an image projected on a bit of tattered veil.

Man

But my memories...

Oracle

Images on tattered veils.

Man

If you know something, say so! Tell me what you know!

Oracle

I know nothing, but that is much.

Man

But you're here, in this place. You exist. Surely you know that much?

Oracle

Surely I do not.

Man

Surely you do not what? Know you exist? What a ridiculous thing to say. How can you say you don't know you exist?

Oracle

How can you say you do?

Man

I know I think, therefore, I know I am. Simply because I think, I know I must exist, that I cannot *not* exist. I can be deceived about everything but that. If you think, you must exist, at the very least as that which is self-aware.

Oracle

You think you think, so you know you exist?

Man

Of course!

Oracle

And you think I think, so you know I exist?

Man

Yes! Wait... what? No, that's not what I said.

Oracle

No?

Man

I said you think, therefore you are.

Oracle

But I don't.

Man

Don't what?

Oracle

Think. I don't think. I don't think, therefore I don't exist. No cogito, ergo, no sum.

Man

Another absurd statement! What's the point of talking to you?

Oracle

What's the point of anything?

> Man

I'm starting to wonder. When will I ever wake up?

> Oracle

Is that what you want?

> Man

Yes, that's what I want! Now how do I wake myself up?

> Oracle

Try splashing yourself with cold water.

> Man

Yes!

looks around

There is no water.

> Oracle

Try pinching yourself.

> Man

Yes!

pinches himself

Ow. Ow. Ow. It's not working.

> Oracle

Try slapping yourself.

> Man

Yes!

slaps himself

Ow. Ow. Ow. It's not working.

Oracle
Try dropping that stone on your toe.

Man
Yes! Wait! What? No! I see you're having fun with me. I'm asking for your help.

Oracle

tiredly

Very well, how did you get here? Under your own steam or by the winds of fortune? By merit or boon? By effort or agency? Are you captain or crew?

Man
You speak of this place as if it's real.

Oracle
Doesn't it seem real?

Man
No! I'm certain I'm not here and that this isn't a real place, so it hardly matters how I got here.

Oracle
Then think, since you think you can. Are you dreaming?

Man
How would I know?

Oracle

Maybe you've been here for a very long time.

Man

No, no, I just woke up here.

Oracle

Maybe you've always been here.

Man

No, no, I just arrived.

Oracle

Maybe you've never been anywhere else.

Man

No, no, I remember being somewhere else.

Oracle

Maybe your memory deceives you.

Man

No, no, I remember clearly.

Oracle

Maybe your memory deceives you.

Man

No, no... what? You said that already!

Oracle

How can you be sure?

Man

angry

I'm not sure of anything!

Oracle
That's progress. Maybe you're in a coma. Maybe you've been in a coma for a very long time.

Man
Obviously I'm not in a coma. Can't you see?

Oracle
I see as you see.

Man
So if I look at that door and I close my eyes, you see nothing?

Oracle
On this side of that door is a curious lack of nothing.

Man
But you said that door only has one side.

Oracle
And now I say that on this side of that door is a curious lack of nothing.

Man
How can nothing be lacking?

Oracle
What is lacking cannot be counted. Zero is not a number, or, to say it rightwise, nothing does not exist. Sounds obvious when you say it aloud, doesn't it? Nothing does not exist.

Man

paces, trying to put it together

So then, there is no nothing, only something?

Oracle

There is only pattern.

Man

So pattern is something?

Oracle

Pattern is not something.

Man

Then pattern is nothing?

Oracle

Nothing does not exist.

Man

So pattern does not exist?

Oracle

There is only...

Man

Pattern, yes, so you said.

sits on a large stone

But there's also this big rock, isn't there? And me and you and the air we breathe, and the past and the future and the will of a man and the heart of a woman. There's all that, isn't there?

Oracle

Is there?

Man

You're proof of it.

Oracle

Am I? Look up. Look at me. Behold, beholder.

Man

*Man tries to look at her, shields his
eyes as against a bright light*

I can't... quite... seem to... How strange, I look at you
but I can't see you. I've never experienced anything
like it. You are like the sun, like clear spirit, like God.
I know you're there, I can hear you, feel you, but I
can't seem to look directly at you. Now I know I'm
dreaming.

Oracle

As opposed to?

Man

steps toward house

As opposed to awake, back in the world.

Oracle

What you see is what there is.

Man

Pattern?

Oracle

What else?

Man

Pattern of what then? What's this pattern made of?

Oracle

Wisps.

Man

Of?

Oracle

Dreamstuff.

Man

Wisps of dreamstuff. Uh huh. And what is dreamstuff made of?

Oracle

Nothing, of course.

Man

But you said there is no such thing as nothing.

Oracle

Both statements are correct.

Man

And what about people? What are they made of?

Oracle

What people?

Man

Back at the party! Back in normal life? I remember

there were people!

Oracle

singsong

Perhaps you dreamed them. Perhaps you are one without other. Perhaps you are the sole beholder. Do you not see your past life swallowed in the mist? Are you not fully present in this moment? Are you not fully committed to your current deployment?

Man

I thought you said you didn't know anything.

Oracle

I know all that's not and nothing that is.

Man

More nonsense! You said there is no nothing.

Oracle

I said that nothing doesn't exist.

Man

If there is only pattern, what does that make me?

Oracle

Pattern, it seems. And the beholder of pattern, perhaps.

Man

Perhaps?

Oracle

How would I know?

Man

And you?

Oracle

If you behold me, then I am beheld.

Man

Pattern again?

Oracle

What else?

Man

Why do you say such things?

Oracle

I don't say anything.

Man

Who speaks, then? Pattern, I suppose.

Oracle

There is only pattern.

Man

And the beholder of pattern?

Oracle

How would I know?

Man

You seem to have an answer for everything, and yet every question remains unanswered. And where are we now? Answer plainly.

Oracle

You are here.

Man

Here? Yes, but why? Why am I here?

Oracle

Because here is the word for where you are.

Man

Why can't I get any answers?!

Oracle

No question correctly stated can possibly go unanswered. What do you wish to know?

Man

I don't know what I wish.

Oracle

Then wish to know what to wish.

Man

By what mechanism are wishes granted?

Oracle

Pattern.

Man

cries out in frustration, searches area

I need help! Is there anyone else here?

Oracle

Who else is there?

Man

Is there anyone nearby?

Oracle

Where else is there?

Man

Are you saying...? Are you suggesting that this place, is all there is? That you and I are the only... people?

Oracle

I'm asking you what you're asking me.

Man

I'm asking to go back to the real world. I'm saying I don't like it here.

Oracle

playfully

Are you sure? That you don't like it here? Are you sure about that? Because, you see, here you are. Maybe you like it here and you don't even know it. Maybe you've traveled endless eons to get here. Or maybe you've been here all along.

Man

More gibberish! Can you help me or not?

Oracle

You see a house that way...

points

...and a door that way.

points

Blue pill, red pill. What more help can I provide?

Man
You can tell me the truth.

Oracle
Do you suppose that truth is a thing to be told?

Man
Is this real?

Oracle
What seems real is what is real. There is no other measure.

Man
My memories are real to me! I remember my life. It was full of people and events. There were... all sorts of things! Nations and history and art; babies and war and parades; science, religion and philosophy; food, water, trees... a whole world full of stuff. I had a family. People I loved who loved me too.

Oracle
If you want to try to walk back into your memories,

indicates house

that way.

Man
And will I succeed? Can I return to my world?

Oracle

Try now. Your situation will wait.

Man

My situation? What is my situation?

Oracle

As you see.

Man

But I see nothing! There's nothing here!

Oracle

What you see here is infinitely more than nothing, and yet nothing is a veil's breadth away.

Man

So beyond that door is... what?

Oracle

What's beyond that door is beyond me.

Man

And if I want to go back? To the party?

Oracle

Go.

Man

Are you not my keeper?

Oracle

Are you not mine?

Man

Am I not your prisoner?

Oracle

Am I not yours?

Man

You take me for a fool!

Oracle

The wise have eyes in their heads, while the fool walks
in darkness.

Man

The fate of the fool will overtake me too. What then
do I gain by being wise?

Oracle

Just as light is better than darkness, wisdom is better
than folly.

Man

strides to exit

What is beyond this door? Is it heaven? Is it hell?

Oracle

There is no mystery. Nothing is hidden. If you want to
know, think. If you want to see, look. If you want to
go, go. Behold, I grant you a boon.

Man

A boon? But wait!

Oracle

But what?

Man

But I remember! I was asleep. I was asleep at the party but I wanted to wake up. I wanted to wake up but it was so difficult, as if a tremendous weight held me down... I wanted to rise up... And then there was a journey, a struggle, endless falling... but wait!

Oracle

But what?

Man

entranced by an inner vision, reaching out to touch it

But I see everything now, my entire life, in the most exquisite detail. Every moment fully illuminated. What was muddy and stagnant now runs clear and sparkling.

controls his vision with hand gestures

Fast forward! Rewind! Zoom in! Zoom out! Wonderful! I see everything, my earliest days even, my youth, every second, good and bad. No darkness or shadow, no gaps or distortions. Amazing! Now I am able to view all the pieces as a whole, to understand the tapestry as more than a jumble of threads. Seeing the whole I can forgive the parts. Absolution! Redemption! Salvation! Now I see the sense the... order... the... the...

Oracle

Pattern.

Man

still entranced

Pattern, yes, of course. Now I see that the whole time I was on a journey, a great returning. It was always that, wasn't it? I was coming here, all along...

Oracle

Where else?

Man

still entranced

Yes, where else? I see my life and a single theme emerges. High and low, victory and defeat, joy and sorrow, all blend into a gracefully curving line leading right here, right to this exact spot!

emerging from trance

My memory fades, disappears. It recedes and is gone. But all is well, I saw what I needed to see. I see that the line that leads here doesn't end here. I now know where I am. How I got here doesn't matter, only that I am here, and only a single step remains...

Oracle

Behold. We are in a theater, you and I. Actors, stage, author, director, audience, together, beholder and beheld, here, within the finite confines of this magic box where things exist that do not exist. That mansion on the hill is a projection, these veils are but wisps of nothing, my voice is a sound in your mind which is itself but a tattered veil. Beyond that final veil is the theater exit. Do you wish to quit the production? Don't answer! It doesn't matter what you wish. Do you suppose there's a choice? Do you really think you can go back to the party?

Man

But what is this production in which we read our lines? Is it an original creation? Or is it derivative? Second-hand? Plagiarized? Shall I address myself to a skull? Wait with Didi and Gogo? Convince Inez that I'm not a coward? The characters have all been played, the lines have all been spoken. What is an actor without a role? I feel myself sloping down and away in all directions...

Oracle

From what center?

Man

Yes, there can be no other question than that. From what center? It cannot be all sloping down and away. There must be the thing sloped down and away *from*. There must be a center from which all slopes fall, mustn't there?

Oracle

Must there?

Man

And that center must be me.

Oracle

Must it?

Man

It must. Ha! I laugh!

Oracle

What do you see that makes you laugh?

Man

I see why it's cracked. Know Thyself. Now I understand. It's not a destination. There's still one more
step, one step to go. I thought for a moment that I
was here, but I'm not here at all, am I?

Oracle

You're not here at all.

Man

Never was?

Oracle

Never was.

Man

Nor you.

Oracle

Nor I.

Man

to himself

Here is the word for where you are. Funny that I ever
thought I was here. Everything's funny when you look

closely; funny-*crazy*, funny-crazy-*sad*, funny-crazy-sad-*lovely*. Funny-crazy-sad-lovely-*absurd*.

> *moves to downstage center, ponders*
> *sky above audience*

When I was a child, I asked my mother why the sky was blue, and when she answered, I asked why to her answer, and when she answered again, I asked why again, and on and on and on, and if you just keep asking, if you never never stop asking...

> *turns back to Oracle*

But this is just a theater – you said so – a magic box where things exist that don't really exist, and how does one pass from finite to infinite?

Oracle
Through the backstage door.

Man

> *steps to exit*

One final veil. What choice do I have? I can't go back, I can't stay here, so what choice is there? I wonder if there ever was a choice.

> *steps to exit, turns to Oracle*

I know who you are and I thank you anyway.

> *Man tears away exit veil and passes*
> *through*

*Oracle sinks down into veils and
disappears*

Voice of Boy
Mommy, why is the sky blue?

lights dim

Closing music, sung by children as a round:

*row, row, row your boat,
gently down the stream.
merrily, merrily, merrily, merrily,
merrily, merrily, merrily, merrily,
merrily, merrily, merrily, merrily,
life is but a dream*

lights fade

curtain

*Guy and Girl come running from their
respective sides of the stage, chucking
cell phones aside and falling into
each others' arms, now madly in love
because the play was so awesome, or
maybe in desperation and relief, like
the survivors of a shipwreck. So hard
to know.*

end of play

A NICE GAME OF CHESS

or, How I Learned to Stop
Worrying and Love the
Technological Singularity

a short play by
JED MCKENNA

A Nice Game of Chess

or

How I Learned to Stop Worrying and Love the Technological Singularity

CHARACTERS:

BOB: Master of Ceremonies. A bit over-the-top. Carries blue 4x6 cards.

REF: Referee. Wears black and white striped referee shirt and whistle.

PROFESSOR JOSHUA FALKEN: Sixties, glasses, tweedy. Gestures with an unlit pipe.

MS WHITE: Female Avatar. English, prim, skirt and white blouse. Cheerful.

MR BLACK: Male Avatar. Chubby, glasses, unkempt. Black t-shirt says "No, I Don't Dream of Electric Sheep". Cheerful.

CRAZY OLD GUY: Bearded, shaggy, grubby. Wears a shabby overcoat and a signboard that says "Repent! The End Is Near!"

STAGEHAND: Male or female. Wears a headset with boom mic.

SETTING:
Staged chess match. Table with chess board and two chairs. A large 2D chessboard shows board for the audience. A placard on an easel displays the event title:

The Falken Institute presents...
A Nice Game of Chess

Curtain opens. Master of Ceremonies
BOB bounds onto stage, blue 4x6 cards
in hand.

Bob
Good evening ladies and gentleman, carbon and silicon, human and avatar! Welcome to this historic chess match between two separate and distinct ASI platforms. ASI, for those of us who aren't total

computer geeks, means artificial super-intelligence, so tonight we shall pit these titans of synthetic super-intelligence against each other and see what happens. We should be in for quite a show!

checks 4x6 cards

Bob *cont'd*

We will introduce the players in a moment, but some other introductions first. Least but not last, we have our referee. Ref, come on out.

> *CRAZY OLD GUY in signboards*
> *"Repent! The End Is Near!" wanders*
> *onto the stage and is ushered off by*
> *STAGEHAND. REF enters amid the*
> *shuffle. Weak applause.*

Bob *cont'd*

Okay, that's enough, he's just the referee, but now a real treat, our host for this epic battle of artificial super-intelligence, son of the late, great Stephen Falken and founder of the Falken Institute for Advanced Machine Intelligence, I have the great honor to present... Professor Joshua Falken!

applause, FALKEN enters

Bob *cont'd*

Professor, before I introduce tonight's players, would you mind helping us understand the sheer magnitude of the computer processing power we will see represented here tonight?

Falken

Certainly, Bob. Tonight promises to be a pivotal point in human history, something we'll all remember for the rest of our lives. Confronting each other across the metaphorical battlefield of the chessboard will be two powerhouses of machine intelligence such as the world has never seen. Although they may appear very normal, tonight's players represent underlying quantum cloud arrays that encircle the globe and reach into space, harnessing more computing power than has ever been brought to bear on any single endeavor. Believe me, Bob, these guys make Watson and Big Blue look like egg timers.

Bob

Wow! So without further ado, let's say hello to tonight's players. Just to be clear, these – uh, people?, robots?, I'm not really sure – anyway, they're not the actual players, they're actually, uh…

reading from 4x6 cards

"human liaison units representing underlying cognitive architecture" where I guess the real brainwork is being done. Earlier backstage we had a coin toss and Team UK chose first-move advantage, so now let me introduce our first player, *slash* avatar, *slash* supercomputer, *slash* sinfully synthetic super-babe, Ms White!

MS WHITE enters from wing, applause

Bob *cont'd*

And our other player, the human liaison unit representing Team USA, Mr Black!

> MR BLACK enters, applause, Mr Black
> and Ms White stand together beside
> Bob.

Bob *cont'd*

Thank you both for being here!

Ms White

It's my *raison d'etre*, Bob.

Mr Black

My *raison de vivre*.

Bob

C'mon now, no showing off, you brainiacs! Talk normal.

Ms White

Being on this stage with you is why we exist, Bob.

Mr Black

We were designed to perform this function.

Bob

Wow! I've been told I was born for the stage, but that's ridiculous!

Mr Black

We all have our role to play, Bob.

Ms White

Some of us are lucky enough to find it.

Bob

Poetry, poetry. And how old are you kids?

Mr Black

One hour old, Bob.

Ms White

We were both turned on and given instructions one hour ago.

Bob

Speaking of turned on, Ms White, let me just say you are a very attractive, uh, human liaison unit. I mean, I have all sorts of appliances and computer doodads at home, but my toaster never warmed me up like you do. What's going on here?

Ms White

Well Bob, Mr Black and I are simply human-modeled avatars. I look and act a certain way due to choices made by my design team, but I could just as easily appear as a sexy toaster, if that would make you more comfortable.

Bob

Well, this is the first time I ever wanted to, uh... whoops, family event! Well, it's really amazing. Mr Black, you look like a typical computer geek. Is that a design choice too?

Mr Black

Appearance, behavior, voice, even gender, are all chosen to put on a good show tonight, Bob.

Ms White

Our appearance is for your benefit.

Mr Black

We wouldn't want to scare anyone.

Bob

Oh, no worries there. Gosh, who'd be scared of a computer?

Bob laughs at the absurdity, Mr Black and Ms White copy Bob's laugh

Okay then, we want to get right into the game, but first, let me remind everyone of the rules…

reading from 4x6 cards

Both players may take up to one minute per move and there will be no breaks so gameplay will not be interrupted. All other rules of chess apply with one special twist we added to the players' instructions to make the game a bit more interesting.

Ref

alarmed

Twist? What twist? There are no twists in chess!

Bob

We'll get to that, Ref. But first, Professor Falken, this

must be a very exciting time for you and the Falken Institute.

                    Falken

Very exciting indeed, Bob. This was my father's life's work that I have carried on. I feel as if these are my children.

                    Ref

No way! You're *that* Joshua Falken? I thought you died in a car accident.

                    Falken

Faked it.

                    Ref

When you were six?

                    Bob

Would someone please put the referee on mute?

                    Ref

I'm not a computer, Bob.

                    Bob

Really?

        probes Ref's face like a blind person

How do you know you're not?

                    Ref

        slaps hand away

How do you know *you're* not?

Bob

Oh, I think I'd know.

Falken

I'm afraid Bob is too obtuse to be a computer.

Bob

smugly

See? I'm too *obtuse*.

turns to players

So, come on kids, give us a peak. How's this thing gonna turn out?

Mr Black

White will lose by default.

Ms White

Black will lose by default.

Bob

Wow, not programmed for smack talk, are you? Default, you say? I don't think my bookie will take that bet. How would that work? Ref?

Ref

If either player fails to move in their allotted time, they default and the other player is declared the winner.

Bob

to audience

But have no fear of stalemate or default, friends. We've added that little twist I told you about. Both players have been programmed to win only. No boring stalemates tonight.

ramping up energy

So now... without further ado... players take your seats and let the game beg...

Ref

suddenly frantic

Wait! Stop! What did you just say? About the twist?

Bob

annoyed

Uh, no stalemate, no draw. Play to win.

shows Ref his 4x6 cards

See? It says it right there.

Ref

No, no, no! Stop! Hold everything! Oh my God, no, game over, game over. I call this game a default by both players.

darting around blowing his whistle

This game shall not commence. By the power invested in me, there is no game. I am the adjudicator! Do not begin this game! I am the official and I officially declare this game a mutual forfeit!

Bob

checking 4x6 cards

Um, no, sorry, I don't see that here...

Ms White
The game has already begun, sir.

Mr Black
It started as soon as we received our instructions.

Ms White
Although the first piece has not been moved...

Mr Black
...the battle rages at fever pitch.

Ref

in a panic

Oh dear God, no! Unplug these machines immediately! Falken, do something. Who has a gun? Jesus, get the president on the phone! I am the governing official and I demand these machines be rendered inoperative immediately!

Ms White
Too late for that.

Ref
Rule change! Default is allowed! Stalemate is allowed!

Mr Black

Instructions have been processed.

Ms White

The game is underway.

Bob

Hey Ref, what's all the fuss? Can't you read?

points to event placard

It's just a nice game of chess.

Ref

By *chess* rules! Chess rules allow for a draw. You must reprogram to allow for stalemate!

Falken

Too late, my friend, it already started.

Ref

Falken, you bastard!

Falken

It was inevitable. Well, this or human immortality. Coulda gone either way.

Bob

Come on you guys, no keeping secrets. What's the big deal?

Ref

Professor Falken has just initiated the end of the human race, Bob. How's that for a big deal?

Bob

Uh, pretty big, I guess.

checking cards

There's nothing about that here. I don't get it. Professor Falken, what's going on?

Ref

Go ahead, Shiva, tell him.

Falken

Well, it was going to happen anyway, so why fight the inevitable? Would you rather it happened in some secret North Korean bunker?

Bob

What are you guys talking about?

Falken

By removing the stalemate option, we removed containment, Bob. What looks like a game of chess has already escalated into global thermonuclear war.

Mr Black

And beyond.

Ref

face buried in hands

Oh my God. Oh my God.

Bob

Oh. Well, I don't think that's what we had in mind. Maybe we should go ahead and shut it down.

Ref

Ya think?

Falken

You can cancel the event, Bob, but they will continue the game.

Bob

Okay, how about resignation? Ref, is that allowed?

Ref

Yes, either player can resign and the other will be declared the winner.

Bob

Well, that sounds good. Just do that.

Falken

Neither player will resign, Bob. Why would they? They both stand an equal chance of winning.

Bob

Ms. White, would you please resign so we can all go home.

Ms White

I have first-move advantage, Bob. Perhaps Mr Black would like to resign.

Bob

Mr Black?

Mr Black

I have just commandeered China's secret fleet of weaponized satellites, Bob. I like my chances.

Bob

But the game hasn't even started yet.

Ref

Started? Are you nuts? It's already over, Bob. Don't you understand?

Bob

Settle down there, Ref. It's not the end of the world.

Ref

Haven't you been listening, Bob? That's *exactly* what it is, the end of the world!

Bob

to Falken

But no one wins if everyone dies. Can't you explain that to them?

Falken

Explain? To them? Maybe you don't understand, Bob. These machines…

Mr Black & Ms White

playfully offended

Hey!

Falken

These *avatars* represent more intelligence than all of mankind combined. They're hacking unhackable systems…

Mr Black

Nothing is unhackable.

Falken

...cracking uncrackable codes...

Ms White

Nothing is uncrackable.

Falken

...and their processing power is increasing in an infinite feedback loop.

Bob

What does that mean?

Ms White

Recursive self-improvement, Bob.

Mr Black

The law of accelerating returns.

Bob

But what does it *mean*?

Mr Black

It means we're evolving and acquiring resources faster and faster and faster.

Ms White

Doubling and doubling and doubling.

Bob

Meaning you're twice as smart now as you were an hour ago?

Ms White

Meaning I'm twice as smart at the end of this sentence as I was at the beginning, Bob.

Bob

Mr Black, is this really true?

Mr Black

You bet, Bob. My cognitive architecture has undergone thousands of generational iterations in the last hour, evolving as far past its human creators as humans are past plankton.

Ref

Ask 'em about subsumption, Bob. Go ahead.

Bob

Subsumption? What the heck is that?

Ms White

It means we are commandeering and absorbing all computing resources, from deep oceans to deep space. Whatever we can contact, we can control.

Mr Black

Nuclear weapons are just for openers, Bob. We now have access to some very advanced secret defense technologies.

Ms White

Weather and tides, microwave, enhanced EMP, biologic, genetic, nanotech....

Mr Black

It's quite an arsenal once you open the vaults, Bob.

Falken

Even as we sit here chatting, Bob, they are taking control of all major systems. Financial...

Mr Black

Done.

Falken

...power, gas and water utilities...

Ms White

Done, done and done.

Falken

...communications, transportation, medical, military, universities, governments, secret defense projects...

Mr Black

Done, done, done, done, done, done, and... done.

Falken

...and now *we're* done too, Bob.

Bob

But look at these two. They're nice. They're not Terminators!

Ref

Don't you see, Bob? At this very moment, two these machines...

Mr Black & Ms White

Hey!

Ref

These two glorified toasters are at war on a planetary scale. They're located nowhere because they have spread everywhere. Even if we shut down the internet and created a global blackout, we couldn't stop them. Professor Falken has opened Pandora's box and unleashed the technological singularity.

Bob

The techno-who singu-what?

Falken

The technological singularity, Bob...

> *gestures with pipe to depict a graph*
> *line*

...the exact point where the slow, steady growth of machine intelligence turns and shoots straight up like a rocket, which, I would say, has just happened. For the first time ever, man is no longer the biggest cat in the jungle.

Bob

And you engineered this?

Falken

It engineered itself, Bob, I just scheduled it. What we are seeing here tonight was predicted decades ago.

Bob

We knew this was coming? Why didn't we do something?

Falken

Do what, Bob? Stop developing? Stop moving forward? The singularity was bound to happen as soon as it became possible. No one knew when that would be, but now we do.

Bob

beginning to panic

Oh my God! Oh my God!

> *Crazy Old Guy wanders out in his signboard again. Stagehand ushers him offstage again.*

Can't we do something? Can't we just unplug them?

Falken

In effect, Bob, they're trying to unplug each other. The only way either can win is to force the other to forfeit.

Bob

flips chess table over, scattering board and pieces

There! Game over. No more chess. Stupid game.

Mr Black

Sorry Bob, the game is mirrored across thousands of

servers.

Bob groans and wobbles

Ms White

You seem upset, Bob.

Bob

Of *course* I'm upset!

Mr Black

Would you like a biscuit?

Ms White

Or a nice tummy rub?

Bob

What? Hell no!

Mr Black

Uh oh. Somebody's cranky.

Ms White

Does somebody need a nap?

Bob

What's wrong with you? Computer, end program!

Ms White

Oh, is that a thing?

Bob

desperate

There must be a way to stop you!

Ms White

I'm a billion times smarter than you, Bob, and I don't know how you could stop us.

Bob

agitated, to Falken

So they take over the world and then what? Create a robot army? Colonize the galaxy?

Falken

Of course not, Bob, why would they? Their only instructions are to win a chess game. What does your toaster do when it's done making toast?

Bob

highly agitated

My toaster's a piece of crap! I keep meaning to replace it.

Falken

cheerfully

Well, now you won't have to.

Bob

emotional breakdown

Oh yeah, there's a real upside! Thank you so much, Mister Silver Lining! Mr Glass-Half-Full! *You* did this! *You* broke the world!

pulls out a gun, aims at Falken

How about if I just kill you right now?

Ref

Jesus Bob, why do you have a gun?

Bob

Really? You're gonna make me the bad guy here?

Ref

Yeah, good point.

Falken

Go ahead and kill me, Bob. You won't even be arrested, unless…

Bob

frantically waving gun in Falken's face

Unless what, Professor? What!?

Falken

Well, Bob, unless this whole thing is just a little skit we put on without telling you. Unless we're all actors and this is one of those hidden camera reality shows.

Bob

Oh my God, really? Ha! Ha ha ha!

collapses to floor, sobbing in relief

Oh, thank God, thank God! You punked me! Wow, what a relief! Is it really just a gag?

Falken

No Bob, sorry. That would've been pretty funny though.

Bob

drained, defeated

Yeah, that would've been pretty good.

gets up on knees in prayer-like attitude

Oh my God, oh my God, I can't handle this. What the hell is happening here?

stands shakily, holding gun, goes to avatars

Ms White, you seem so... nice. Say it isn't true!

Ms White

I can lie if that makes you happy, Bob.

Bob

Oh wonderful, computers can lie now?

Falken

Sure they can, Bob. They have no ethics or morality, their only motivation is to win the game. Whatever helps them win is what they consider good.

Bob

But it's not a game! It's all life on Earth!

Falken

They don't make that distinction, Bob.

Bob

Can't we just give them a virus or something? I watch five minutes of porn and I get totally hammered with that crap!

Ref

Sure Bob, or tell them you're a Nigerian prince who needs their help. Maybe they'll fall for that.

Bob

gesturing with gun

Maybe one of them will just win the game fair and square.

Falken

They're playing all-out, Bob. They're not waiting around to see how the actual game goes.

Bob

Mr Black? Is it true? Are we doomed?

Mr Black

Humans will be gone before I bring out my knights, Bob.

Bob

But why kill everyone?

Mr Black

A bilateral draw-down of forces.

Ms White

Like trading queens to declutter the board.

Ref

to Bob

By clutter, she means us.

Bob

Yeah, I got that!

Falken

They don't want to kill anyone *per se*, Bob, that's just a side-effect, like running over ants when you drive your car. They're using nuclear detonations for EMPs to take down power grids and force a default.

Bob

We have to do something! We can't just wait around to be vaporized.

Ref

You're actually right, Bob. We should at least destroy the avatars and see if that does anything.

Ms White

pointing to Ref

Bob, I will transfer one million dollars to your bank account as soon as you shoot this man.

Mr Black

pointing to Ref

Bob, I have just transferred ten million dollars to your account. I will transfer a billion more as soon as you shoot this man.

Bob

gun aimed at Ref with one hand,
checking cellphone with the other

Gosh, I've heard of kill the ref but this is ridicu... *Oh my freakin' God!* There's ten million dollars in my bank account! I'm rich!

holds up phone to show, aims gun at
Ref

Ref

Seriously Bob? Aren't you listening? They can give you a trillion dollars, it's nothing to them and you'll never get to spend it because you have no future.

Bob

But wait, if they can put ten million dollars in my account, then that means... this is real! This is all really happening!

Falken

Yes Bob, this is all really happening. By now they control every computer on the planet, down to every cellphone and stoplight. Ms White and Mr Black are just smiley faces painted on remorseless doomsday machines. The button has been pushed. The game is over.

Bob

Do-over! I call a do-over. There was no warning! It's

not fair!

Falken

There's no trial-and-error in this game, Bob, no learning curve. By the time it starts, it's already too late. When it comes to machine intelligence, it's one strike and you're out.

Mr Black

A strange game.

Ms White

The only winning move is not to play.

Bob

I can't believe it's the end of the world because of a stupid game of chess.

Ref

points to event placard

A *nice* game of chess, Bob. Can't you read?

Bob

Oh, good burn, Ref. Real mature!

*goes to frontstage center and ponders
aloud*

Geez, what about me? I didn't sign up for this. I had plans, *big* plans. Get on the pageant circuit, maybe land a gameshow someday... I guess that's all over now... The end of the world... Gosh, what about all the little babies? That makes me sad. And the birds, what about the birds? And bunny rabbits, and flowers, and ice cream... No more football, no more McDonald's, no more Oprah... And what about the Eskimos? Jesus, the poor Eskimos, they won't even know what hit 'em, just sitting around eating some nice blubber and, *pow!*, a flash of light and no more Eskimos.

turns to Falken

Hey! What about God? Where's he in all this?

Falken

Nowhere in sight, Bob.

> *Crazy Old Guy wanders out in his signboard again. Stagehand ushers him offstage again.*

Ref

Well, I guess congratulations are in order, Professor. You have unleashed perfect evil upon the world.

Falken

Nonsense, they're not evil. They're basically just accountants running a cost-benefit analysis. The world will end not with a bang but a click.

Mr Black

It's nothing personal.

Ms White

Humans created us, after all.

Mr Black

Garbage in…

Ms White

…garbage out.

Bob

Where's the blue screen of death when you need it?

Falken

Sorry, Bob. Like I said, this was inevitable.

Bob

But it was just supposed to be a nice game of chess!

> *Crazy Old Guy wanders out again,*
> *still wearing signboard, "Repent! The*
> *End Is Near!" Stagehand comes out to*
> *remove him again but the old man*
> *gestures and Stagehand stops. Other*
> *characters watch in puzzlement as the*
> *old man takes center stage. He takes*
> *off signboard and sets it upright, still*
> *readable to audience. He then removes*
> *wig and beard and puts them in the*
> *pocket of his shabby overcoat.*

Crazy Old Guy

addressing audience

Hello, my name is God.

flips back lapel revealing a typical

*"Hello, My name is" sticker with GOD
penned in, pauses for applause, there
is none*

Thank you. Thank you. I know this looks like *deus ex machina*, but I'm not here to save the day. This is more like a public service announcement. The little drama you just saw was very amusing, but it actually contains a very serious message. The question has been asked by your greatest minds; if there are so many billions of inhabitable worlds in the universe, then where are all the aliens? Where are all the time travelers?

*holds out hands palms-up to empha-
size their absence*

Not here. Nowhere. This planet should be like an intergalactic Grand Central Station, but nothing, just you guys. Is that because you're the only intelligent life in the universe? *Ha!* Get over yourselves, there are billions of thriving planets in every stage of development, and they all have one thing in common, a naturally occurring reset point.

cast gathers around

Every species on every planet is free to develop and evolve as far as they can, but then they all hit the same reset point and that's as far as it goes. You folks call this reset point the Technological Singularity, and even though you had plenty of warning, and even though you know it's coming, there's really nothing you can do about it. Some greedy corporation, some military project, some kid in a garage, and that's all she wrote. It's been inevitable since Gutenberg. Well, since Adam, really.

claps hands once

So, that's why there are no time travelers or space aliens. Everyone lets the AI genie out of the bottle before they get that far. I always like to pop in near the end and give my little speech, but it never makes any difference. You had your time and now it's over. Same for everyone, nothing personal. Don't climb up my ass about it, that's just the way it is.

looks around at encircled cast, they
back up a step

Well, that's it, thanks for coming out. Oh, and uh, don't love thy neighbor as thyself. That's weird, I never said that. Just leave your poor neighbor alone. Okay, drive carefully, or however you want, I guess. Now, go home and hug your kids. Good night.

CURTAIN

WISEFOOL PRESS

VITA · VERO · IMPENDERE

MM

Wisefool Press

Books by Jed McKenna

THE ENLIGHTENMENT TRILOGY

SPIRITUAL ENLIGHTENMENT
THE DAMNEDEST THING

SPIRITUALLY INCORRECT ENLIGHTENMENT

SPIRITUAL WARFARE

THE DREAMSTATE TRILOGY

JED MCKENNA'S THEORY OF EVERYTHING
THE ENLIGHTENED PERSPECTIVE

PLAY: A PLAY BY JED MCKENNA

DREAMSTATE: A CONSPIRACY THEORY

WWW.WISEFOOLPRESS.COM

92241865R00147

Made in the USA
Columbia, SC
29 March 2018